The Great British Limerick Book

BY THE SAME AUTHOR

The Scottish Limerick Book - Filthy Limericks for Every Town in Scotland

BY THE SAME AUTHOR (BUT ABSOLUTELY, CATEGORICALLY NOTHING REMOTELY LIKE THE GREAT BRITISH LIMERICK BOOK OR THE SCOTTISH LIMERICK BOOK)

Scott Walker: The Rhymes of Goodbye

A Generation of Change, a Lifetime of Difference? British Social Policy since 1979 (with Martin Evans)

The Great British Limerick Book

Filthy Limericks for (Nearly) Every Town in the UK

Lewis Williams

First published in the United Kingdom in 2015
Reprinted with minor revisions 2016

By Corona Books UK

www.coronabooks.com

ISBN 978-0-9932472-0-0

Cover design by Colourburst
www.colourburst.com

INTRODUCTION

There was a young man from Devizes
Whose bollocks were different sizes
One was so small
It was no ball at all
But the other was big and won prizes

The rhymes collected in this volume are the result of many years of painstaking research. Indeed the project began in 1993 when I met a man whose testicles were quite extraordinary, one being somewhat larger than the other. We struck up a friendship and hit upon the scheme of using his larger testicle to our financial advantage. The number of prizes actually awarded for large testicles being somewhat limited in the mid-1990s, we embarked on various ruses such as passing off his larger testicle as an enormous gooseberry in order to win prizes at village fêtes up and down the country. Happily the man came from Devizes and so circumstances lent themselves very nicely to a rhyme about him.

Unfortunately one day our plans backfired when someone decided to take a large bite out of the 'prize gooseberry' in question. After this unfortunate incident I parted company with the man from Devizes and wondered if I might be able to meet other people about whom rhymes could be written. So began a quest to travel the length and breadth of the country visiting every town and seeking out people like the man with remarkable testicles whose qualities, habits, stories and location might lend themselves to filthy limericks. The results are before you.

Any suggestions that I have simply filled the book up by using similar limericks for similar sounding place names or by using the 'Reg' limerick when I couldn't come up with a decent rhyme are entirely without foundation. It is for example purely by coincidence that I met three men with exceptional penises that came from Matlock, Baldock and Tavistock. And it is also through a series of remarkable coincidences that I met a number of men called Reg all of whom had been castrated by their wives after being caught *in flagrante delicto* and all of whom came from places with names that are really hard to find rhymes for.

It's been a long journey and I hope you enjoy the book. My only regret is that, alas, the New England town of Nantucket is not in Great Britain.

Lewis Williams

CONTENTS

Note: In order to give the book 'chapters' of roughly equal size across the four countries that make up the UK, current administrative accuracy has been partially sacrificed and the device adopted of organising Scottish limericks by the old system of regions and Welsh limericks by ceremonial county.

Scotland

Limericks from ...

England

Limericks from ...

Wales

Limericks from ...

Northern Ireland

Limericks from ...

Index of Towns

Scotland

Borders

Coldstream

There was a young man from Coldstream
Whose carelessness was quite extreme
Whilst brushing in haste
He confused his toothpaste
With his grandfather's haemorrhoid cream

Duns

There once was a young man from Duns
Whose balls were like two Chelsea buns
But if their size was impressive
Their weight was excessive
As each one weighed nearly two tons

Galashiels

Once two brothers from Galashiels
Were put through some dreadful ordeals
By a dominatrix
Who stamped on their pricks
Then did it again in high heels

Hawick

In Hawick in the Scottish Borders
There's a club of *Razzle* magazine hoarders
Who collect every issue
And wrap them in tissue
And wank over them in different orders

Kelso

I stripped naked one night in Kelso
And ran round to put on a show
First preparing my knob
With a fairly big blob
Of fluorescent paint to make it glow

Newtown St. Boswells

A young man from Newton St. Boswells
On the end of his dick, tied some bells
Which chimed to perfection
When he got an erection
And CDs of the tunes he now sells

Peebles

From my night out in Peebles, Borders
I recall well the bar at last orders
But I just don't remember
What I did with my member
That got me served with three court orders

Selkirk

There was a young man from Selkirk
With quite an odd physical quirk
Whenever he'd see
A nice cup of tea
His penis would suddenly perk

Central

Alloa

There was a young lady from Alloa
Whose boyfriend was a famous fruit grower
She bragged to her chums
About the size of his plums
And the stalk that he'd quite often show her

Bo'ness

At Tesco's in the town of Bo'ness
With, I might say, a degree of finesse
I was showing my chopper
To a fellow shopper
And she gave it a gentle caress

Denny

There once was a young man from Denny
Who was born with a bollock too many
Though some people would scoff
He was much better off
Than his brother who hadn't got any

Falkirk

There was a young man from Falkirk
Whose penis one day went berserk
And came everywhere
With litres to spare
Then twitched with a curious jerk

Grangemouth

In Grangemouth there's an oil refinery
A port, a canal and a winery
And to thrill you to bits
All the girls have 10 tits
That is if you count them in binary

Larbert

The young lady I met in Larbert
Had breasts that were lovely and pert
I told her as much
As she fondled my crutch
And I knew I was on a dead cert

Muckhart

An explosion occurred in Muckhart
When a camper set light to a fart
And was so flatulent
It blew up his tent
Then tore the whole campsite apart

Stenhousemuir

There was a chap from Stenhousemuir
Whose ejaculations were premature
Till he hit on this thing
To tie his balls up with string
And razor wire just to make sure

Stirling

There was a young lady from Stirling
Who could set her nipples a-twirling
For this trick with her tits
She'd charge you two bits
Or thirty-five pence in pounds sterling

Tullibody

There was a young man from Tullibody
Whose habits were really quite odd, he
Could only get aroused
If he put on a blouse
And listened to Showaddywaddy

Dumfries and Galloway

Annan*

There once was a young man from Annan
Who was blown down the street by a cannon
The force of the blast
Blew his balls up his ass
And his penis to the River Shannon

Castle Douglas*

A young lady from Castle Douglas
Used a dynamite stick as a phallus
They found her vagina
In North Carolina
And her arsehole in Buckingham Palace

Dalbeattie

There was a young lady from Dalbeattie
Who according to local graffiti
She had no holes barred
If you had some lard
And promised to call her a sweetie

Dumfries*

There was a young lady from Dumfries
Whose muff hair hung down to her knees
The crabs in her mott
Tied the hair in a knot
And constructed a flying trapeze

Gretna*

A young lady from Gretna Green
Crept into the vestry unseen
She pulled down her knickers
And likewise the vicars
And said 'How's about it old bean?'

Kirkcudbright

There was a chap from Kirkcudbright†
Whose bollocks were a sight to see
They were square not round
And each one weighed a pound
And on top of all that he had three

Stranraer

There was a young man from Stranraer
Who had ambitions to be a porn star
He caused quite some fuss
At the Jobcentre Plus
Showing the asset that might take him far

---

† Pronounced 'Kirk-koo-bree'

Fife

Benarty

There was a pirate from Ben-arty
Who said to me, 'Ah ha me hearty
Well by any means
I enjoyed all those beans
But they've left me most terribly farty'

Buckhaven

At the town parade once in Buckhaven
I was cautioned for my misbehaving
It was such a nice day
I got carried away
And my dick in my hand I was waving

Cowdenbeath

There was a whore from Cowdenbeath
Who offered cheap oral relief
But despite the low price
You'd not come back twice
On account of her rather sharp teeth

Cupar

There was a young lady from Cupar
Who I thought was really quite super
Just one look down her blouse
Would have me aroused
And she'd wank me off into a stupor

Dalgety Bay

An old man from Dalgety Bay
Took his testicles round on a tray
Saying, 'Look at their size
I'm offering a prize
For the first one to guess what they weigh'

Dunfermline

A contest was held in Dunfermline
That the person pissing farthest would win
I surpassed the whole nation
At such urination
When my stream of piss reached Dublin

Glenrothes

There was a chap from Glenrothes, Fife
Who bought himself a mail order wife
And though he wasn't fussy
She hadn't a pussy
And her cock gave him the shock of his life

Kirkcaldy

At the library one day in Kirkcaldy[†]
I said to them, 'Oh lordy lordy
With *The Perfumed Garden*
I couldn't get one hard-on
Have you got something slightly more bawdy?'

Lochgelly

I met a dominatrix from Lochgelly
Who fair turned my knees into jelly
When she set about my cock
With a big lump of rock
My screams could be heard in New Delhi

Methil*

There was a young man from Methil
Who swallowed a dynamite pill
His heart retired
His bum backfired
And his willy shot over the hill

Rosyth

There once was a man from Rosyth
Who bought himself a mail order wife
But he regretted his punt
When he couldn't find her cunt
And her cock gave him the shock of his life

---

† Pronounced 'Kirk-caw-dee'

St Andrews

At St Andrews once on the golf course
My partner took a shot with such force
He clipped my meat and two veg
With the back swing of his wedge
For which he showed quite some remorse

Grampian

Aberdeen*

A young man from Aberdeen, he
Once spilt gin all over his weenie
Just to be couth
He added vermouth
And slipped his girlfriend a martini

Buckie

While stood at a urinal in Buckie
A man said to me, 'Excuse me, ducky
That dick in your hand
Looks rather grand
In comparison I feel quite unlucky'

Elgin

There was a young lady from El-gin
Who thought sex would be a mortal sin
But if no one was looking
She'd think nothing of fucking
Herself with a big rolling pin

Ellon

There was a young lady from Ellon
Who had one most enormous melon
So her other breast
Was quite second best
And didn't look much like a well 'un

Forres

Said a husband to his wife from Forres
'I've read your magazines again, Doris
But I'm not really a fan
Of *Cosmopoli-tan*
And what's the thing they call a cli-toris?'

Fraserburgh

Fraserburgh is known for its shellfish
But when I screwed there this lady called Trish
The crabs that I caught
Were not of the sort
You would serve in a fine dining dish

Inverurie

Once in the town of Inverurie
I was wanking away with a fury
On the top deck of a bus
Which caused quite a fuss
And I ended up facing a jury

Peterhead

Once in the town of Peterhead
I was wanking away in this bed
But it was on the top floor
Of a furniture store
And again to my arrest this led

Portlethen

And one time in Portlethen town
I was stroking my dick up and down
In a branch of Barclays Bank
But was arrested mid-wank
Which quite changed my smile to a frown

Stonehaven

One time in the town of Stonehaven
I gave into this curious craving
And started pulling my pud
In the middle of a pub
And was cautioned for such misbehaving

Highland

Dingwall*

There was a young man from Dingwall
Whose arsehole was no good at all
When he sat down to poo
It went all askew
And shot all his shit up the wall

Fort William

To Fort William near to Glen Coe
I went once with plenty of dough
But met this high-class hooker
Who was such a fine looker
I blew all my cash in one go

Inverness

At the vicar's party in Inverness
The requirement was for fancy dress
But I caused quite a shock
Going dressed as a cock
And the evening was not a success

John o' Groats

There was a young man from John o' Groats
Who was yet to have his first oats
And at age thirty-three
Still had his virginity
Unless you count the times he fucked goats

Kingussie

There was a young lady from Kingussie[†]
With an amazing musical pussy
It'd play for a starter
A Beethoven sonata
Then several works by Debussy

Skye

When I was on the Isle of Skye
I overdid the old Spanish fly
I had a stiff member
From the fourth of December
Till Friday the tenth of July

Tain

I found out in the small town of Tain
Sexual practice was far from mundane
One particular group
Formed a curious loop
That I understand is called a monk's chain

[†] Which is pronounced 'King-ewsie' and therefore this limerick may
require a particular pronunciation of the word 'pussy'!

Tobermory

The night that I stayed in Tobermory
It was a varied political story
I early on kissed
A Scottish Nationalist
But then shagged a Green and a Tory

Wick

There once was a young man from Wick
Who could give his own penis a lick
At most social functions
He'd have no compunction
About showing the party this trick

Lothian

Bathgate

There was a young man from Bathgate
Who went fishing with his dick as bait
An idea unwise
But to his surprise
He caught four eels, a cod and a skate

Bonnyrigg

There was a young lady from Bonnyrigg
Who was very fond of having a frig
With dildoes by the number
Or courgette or cucumber
Or anything phallic and big

Broxburn

There once was young man from Broxburn
Who at a whorehouse was waiting in turn
When he spotted his mother
Who was serving another
Which gave him a spot of concern

Dalkeith

There once was a whore from Dalkeith
Who was so accomplished at hand relief
That whatever you'd planned
You'd come in her hand
Before you got near her curtains of beef

Dunbar

At my stall at the fete in Dunbar
I sold jams and preserves by the jar
But the sales of little pots
Each containing two shots
Of my pearl jam didn't go very far

Edinburgh

A man from Edinburgh, Scotland's capital
Went for forty days without a crap at all
Then when he went to the loo
He produced so much poo
The toilet bowl didn't quite trap it all

Linlithgow

With this young lady in Linlithgow
My performance was quite a poor show
My dick wouldn't rise
But it had been unwise
To first drink five pints of Bordeaux

Livingston

Once in the town of Living-ston
I went to a beauty salon
But wanted my money back
On their back, sac and crack
As they'd left half my pubic hair on

Musselburgh

I met a young lady from Musselburgh
Who told me that I mustn't hustle her
But that it might arouse her
If I had in my trousers
A reasonably decent love muscle there

Penicuik

There was a young man from Penicuik[†]
Who had once read a medical book
And although he'd insist
'I'm no gynaecologist'
He'd be happy to take a good look

Whitburn

There was a young lady from Whitburn
Who once had a peculiar turn
At the botanical garden
She said, 'I beg your pardon'
Then pissed on their fragrant wood fern

---

† Pronounced 'Pennycook'

23

Shetland and Orkney

Kirkwall

There was a young man from Kirkwall
Who had quite a terrible fall
On some very sharp rock
Which sliced off his cock
And left him too missing a ball

Lerwick*

There was once a girl from Lerwick
Who said to her mum, 'What's a dick?'
She said, 'My dear Annie,
It goes in your fanny
And jumps up and down till it's sick'

Stromness

There was a young lady from Stromness, Orkney
Who set about trying to stalk me
But she needed no persistence
As I put up no resistance
And quite easily would let her pork me

Strathclyde

Airdrie

There was a young man from Airdrie
Who was bit on his dick by a flea
His date that night was botched
As he scratched at his crotch
And wailed like a howling banshee

Ayr

There once was a young man from Ayr
Whose sex doll had real pubic hair
But whilst at her furry cup
He'd have to blow her up
As she needed a puncture repair

Barrhead

There was a young man from Barrhead
Who kept several corpses in bed
Saying, 'My necrophilia
Is getting much sillier
I must find a live one instead'

Bearsden

At A&E to a chap from Bearsden
They said, 'What is it this time, then?
We'll give you some verbal
If it's a bloody gerbil
You've got stuck up your arse once again'

Clydebank

There was an artist from Clydebank
Who died with nothing in the bank
And left as an estate
Just a few self-portraits
Each depicting him having a wank

Cumbernauld

There was a young man from Cumbernauld
Whose manners were quite uncontrolled
He once got out his pecker
On a crowded double decker
And shouted out, 'Who wants a hold?'

Dumbarton*

A flatulent actor from Dumbarton
Led a life exceedingly spartan
Till a playwright one day
Wrote a well-received play
With a part for the actor to fart in

East Kilbride

There was a chap from East Kilbride
Who was caught with his bit on the side
He was asked by his wife
Who was holding a knife
'Do you want your balls grilled or fried?'

Glasgow

There was a young lady Glaswegian
Who was famed for her pubic region
Her twat was so huge
It became a refuge
And an outpost for the French Foreign Legion

Greenock

I called on my lady friend from Green-ock
And she said to me, 'How have you been cock?
Now that you've called round
Quick get your trousers down
It's been at least two days since I've seen cock'

Hamilton

There was a farmer from Hamil-ton
Who when he'd slayed a pig, waste he would shun
He'd eat every part
From its kidneys to heart
And its dick in a frankfurter bun

Irvine

A widowed old lady from Irvine
Thought her husband's dick worth preserving
And even went as far
As to display it in a jar
Which her house guests found somewhat unnerving

Johnstone

There was a young chef from Johnstone
Who was terribly accident prone
He gave himself some cuts
And sliced off both his nuts
When a chicken he was trying to debone

Kilmarnock

There was a young man from Kilmar-nock
With a strange manner of taking stock
On alternate Mondays
He'd check in his undies
To make sure he had two balls and a cock

Kilwinning

By the time I reached the town of Kilwinning
I'd been through an A to Z of sinning
Without anything new
There was fuck all else to do
Than to start again at the beginning

Kirkintilloch

On the day I was in Kirkintilloch
I ran to the top of a hillock
And got my knob out
And waved it about
It was said I behaved like a pillock

Motherwell

At a second hand shop in Motherwell
A sports jacket they tried to me sell
Saying, 'It's a bargain find
That is if you don't mind
The semen stain on the lapel'

Paisley

I was caught by this fellow from Paisley
In the act fucking his wife like crazy
But he said, 'Here's ten bob
You've saved me a job
I'd screw her myself but I'm lazy'

Prestwick

There was a young man from Prestwick
Who always came a little too quick
Till in measures quite drastic
He tied his balls with elastic
And used dry ice to numb up his dick

Renfrew

Said a young man who came from Renfrew
'This bestiality I must eschew
My last three girlfriends
All had very nice ends
But all had four legs and went moo'

Rothesay

An old man from Rothesay, Bute
Did his laundry in his birthday suit
Till he let his dick dangle
And it went in the mangle
And caused him a pain quite acute

Rutherglen

There was a young lady from Rutherglen
For whom sex had been beyond her ken
Till she met an instructor
Who taught her and fucked her
And she couldn't get enough of it then

Saltcoats*

There was a young lady from Saltcoats
Who had sex with twenty-five goats
And when she was through
She had a cold brew
And wrote them all nice thank you notes

Troon*

There was a young man from Troon
Whose farts could be heard on the moon
When least you'd expect 'em
They'd burst from his rectum
With the force of a raging typhoon

Tayside

Arbroath

A vicar there was from Arbroath
Was once heard to mutter an oath
When attacked by some badgers
That went for his nadgers
And unfortunately bit off them both

Carnoustie

In the small Scottish town of Carnoustie
To some strange habits they introduced me
I'd never seen such a thing
As their bondage sling
And to tears I admit it reduced me

Dundee[*]

There was an old man from Dundee
Who had sex with an ape in a tree
The results were quite horrid
All ass and no forehead
Three balls and a purple goatee

Forfar

To the doctor I said, 'It's pathetic
Those pills were a strong diuretic
I don't mean to be quibbling
But I've not seen such bad dribbling
Since I last watched Forfar Athletic'

Killiecrankie

A young lady from Killiecrankie
Was dead keen for some hanky panky
She aroused me so surely
I came prematurely
And alas she got really quite cranky

Kinross

The pornography I bought from Kinross
Was frankly an utter dead loss
It was hardly top drawer
And very softcore
And I couldn't even manage one toss

Monifieth

A young lady from Monifieth
Told me something quite beyond belief
That her vagina could speak
Well, I gave it a week
But all I heard from it was a queef

Montrose

There was an old man from Montrose
Who quite often his dick would expose
Especially when swimming
He'd annoy all the women
By pulling up and down his Speedos

Perth

When in Perth on the River Tay
I went to a BDSM soiree
And despite my complaints
Their bondage restraints
Left my balls aching all the next day

Stobswell

I asked the doctor from Stobswell
If he could tell me if my Uncle Bob's well
He said for an answer
'It's testicular cancer
But on the positive side, though, his knob's well'

Western Isles

Western Isles*

A boatman from the Western Isles
Suffered severely from piles
He couldn't sit down
Without a deep frown
So he had to row standing for miles

Harris

There once was a young man from Harris
Who cast his dick in plaster of paris
He put it on a stand
And thought it looked grand
On the dashboard of his Toyota Yaris

Stornoway

With this lass in the town of Stornoway
Something happened to quite take my horn away
I had a mishap
With my Arab strap
Which left half my pubic hair torn away

Uist

Waking early one day in Uist
I fancied a quick one off the wrist
But I didn't come soon
And when it got to noon
I decided I'd better desist

England

Bedfordshire

Ampthill

There was a young man from Ampthill
Whose bollocks were feeling the chill
But his plan quite unwise
Brought tears to his eyes
When he warmed them up under the grill

Bedford*

A Bedford man who was named Reg
Was screwing this lass in a hedge
When along came his wife
With a big carving knife
And cut off his meat and two veg

Biggleswade

There once was a whore from Biggleswade
Who was forced to abandon her trade
Though a really good screw
Her problem was due
To her forgetting to ask to get paid

Dunstable

There was a young man named Runstable
Who walked through the streets of Dunstable
With his cock hanging out
He'd wave it about
Until he got caught by a constable

Dunstable Downs

A young lady from Dunstable Downs
Had tits that weighed ninety-nine pounds
She searched near and far
In vain for a bra
That would stop them from hitting the ground

Flitwick

There was a young man from Flitwick
Who could do an extraordinary trick
He'd play all sorts of tunes
With the use of two spoons
That he'd strap to the side of his dick

Houghton Regis

Said a masochist from Houghton Re-gis
'I know most blokes would give it a miss
But whacking my cock
With this stainless steel wok
Is truly my idea of bliss'

Kempston*

The nipples on this lass from Kemps-ton
When aroused, were twelve inches long
This embarrassed her lover
Who was pained to discover
She expected no less from his dong

Leighton Buzzard

A nudist from Leighton Buz-zard
Was barbecuing out in his yard
When in error, most barmy
Cooked his own salami
Leaving his manhood quite charred

Linslade

Once in the town of Linslade
There lived a very fair maid
Who'd charge just ten bob
For a lovely hand job
But five hundred pounds to get laid

Luton

I once went to a bed-shop in Luton
With nothing but my birthday suit on
I always get undressed
Before having a rest
And I wanted to try out a futon

Potton*

There once was a young man from Potton
Who feared that his knob had gone rotten
He said, 'Zut alors
It's all covered in sores
From all the VD that I've gotten'

Sandy

There was a young lady from Sandy
Who quite often would come in handy
Though not a hooker
Or much of a looker
She'd do it for one half of shandy

Wixams

There once was a young man from Wixams
Who suffered some dreadful afflictions
That ranged from a cough
To his knob falling off
And were worse than his doctor's predictions

Woburn

There was a young man from Woburn
Who once tried to fuck a tea urn
But what he forgot
Was the thing was still hot
And his knob got a third degree burn

Berkshire

Ascot

There was a young man from Ascot
Who could tie up his dick in a knot
As a much bigger trick
He once used his dick
To moor up a luxury yacht

Bracknell

There was a young man from Brack-nell
Who on his own penis would dwell
He'd unbutton his flies
And measure its size
On the hour and the half hour as well

Crowthorne

There was an old chap from Crowthorne
With ambition to star in some porn
But it wasn't to be
As 1983
Was the last time that he had the horn

Earley

There once was a young man from Earley
Whose manner was always quite surly
When accidently castrated
He was less than elated
But it made him a little more girly

Eton

In a pissing contest held in Eton
I pissed really far and won Heat One
But in the second heat
When a chap pissed fifty feet
I knew I was pretty well beaten

Hungerford

In Hungerford on the River Dun
Playing cricket one day in the sun
It was a school of hard knocks
As I'd forgot my box
And the ball caught me in the left plum

Maidenhead

There was a young man from Maidenhead
Who put on his dick margarine spread
But he was heard to utter
'I'd much prefer butter
Or perhaps some beef dripping instead'

Newbury*

A young lady from Newbury, Berks†
Said, 'It's more fun indoors than in parks
You feel more at ease
Your ass doesn't freeze
And by-passers don't make snide remarks'

Reading

There once was a 'brit milah' in Reading
Where instead of a foreskin shedding
The old circumcisist
Had first got himself pissed
And gave the boy's cock a good shredding

Sandhurst

There was a young man from Sandhurst
Whose fate was peculiarly cursed
If he ever saw some shit
He'd fall into it
And usually do so headfirst

Slough

There was a young man from Slough
Who wanted to, but didn't know how
He asked a farmer
'If I promise not to harm her
Could I have a practice run with your cow?'

---

† Which can be pronounced 'Berks' to rhyme with 'jerks' (as in the rhyming slang that gives us 'Berk' from 'Berkshire Hunt') or perhaps more commonly, as we have it here, 'Barks' to rhyme with 'parks'

Thatcham

There once was a young man from Thatcham
Who took out his bollocks to scratch 'em
Saying, 'They're lovely and round
And weigh half a pound
I'll bet yours just cannot quite match 'em'

Windsor

Windsor is known for its knot
And also the castle it's got
But a lesser known fact
Is it's where I did contract
My first case of raging knob-rot

Wokingham

Some pals on a day trip to Wokingham
Were after some whores to be poking 'em
But on finding none
Instead for some fun
They took out their cocks and were stroking 'em

Woodley

To his girlfriend a young man from Woodley
Said, 'Cunnilingus with you suits me goodly
But my face has a rash
From the love of your gash
Could you keep it a little less stubbly?'

Buckinghamshire

Amersham

There was a lass from Amersham
Who covered her twat with plum jam
She was quite surprised
At the number of flies
It brought there to swarm round her clam

Aylesbury

In Aylesbury they have this strange duck
You might like to go take a look
But on the other hand
If you've better things planned
You probably won't give a fuck

Beaconsfield

In Beaconsfield the home of Disraeli
A masochist told me that daily
He got a big kick
From whacking his dick
With the blunt end of his ukulele

Buckingham

There was a young lady from Buckingham
Who really liked dicks and fucking 'em
She had no fear
If they went up her rear
But she then drew the line at sucking 'em

Burnham

There was a young man from Burnham
Who loathed open fires and would spurn 'em
He'd an unnatural fear
That if he stood too near
The fire might catch his bollocks and burn 'em

Chesham

In the town of Chesham, Bucks
I once found some interesting books
One most delightful
And indeed quite insightful
Showed a thousand positions of fucks

High Wycombe

One day in High Wycombe, Bucks
I asked all and sundry for fucks
But throughout the town
I just got turned down
Till I got lucky once in Starbucks

Marlow

There once was a lass from Mar-low
Who would put on a bargain strip show
Or if you would rather
A spot of how's your father
Well that was just two pounds a go

Milton Keynes

A young man from Milton Keynes
Was a little too keen on his beans
He'd have them for brunch
And breakfast and lunch
Then do musical farting routines

Newport Pagnell

In Newport Pagnell I lost my bag
Which turned out to be quite a drag
I lost a battery charger
My penis enlarger
And my very best porno mag

Olney*

There was a young man from Ol-ney
Who tried to piss over a tree
The tree was too high
And it fell in his eye
And now the poor bugger can't see

Princes Risborough

I was strip-searched in Princes Ris-borough
And the police there were extremely thorough
I didn't expect 'em
To look up my rectum
And my expression was quite one of horror

Wendover

A young lady from Wendover
Was quite the easy legover
On the strength of one dance
She'd pull down her pants
Turn right round for you and bend over

Winslow

There was a young lady from Winslow
Whose tits hung particularly low
She'd never go far
Without a strong bra
Or she'd trip on them on the word 'go'

Woburn Sands

A young lady from Woburn Sands
Had extraordinary mammary glands
The size of her tits
Would thrill you to bits
Just her nipples were the size of your hands

Cambridgeshire

Cambridge

In Cambridge by the River Cam
The Queen showed me her bearded clam
In order to be nice
I overlooked the pubic lice
And said, 'It's a very nice one, Ma'am'

Chatteris

There once was a man from Chatteris
Always careless when having a piss
Till his wife said, 'That's final
I'll buy you a urinal
And I'll kill you if you still fucking miss'

Ely

There was a young lady from Ely
Who went to see a doctor named Deeley
He gave her some pills
Said to cure all her ills
But all they did was made her pee freely

Godmanchester

In Godmanchester town by the Ouse
My virginity there I did lose
At age thirty-eight
I'd left it quite late
And I rang Mum to tell her the news

Huntingdon

At a fete they held in Huntingdon
I helped them to get their bunting done
I hung some from a tree
But I fell and broke my knee
Which I have to say wasn't much cunting fun

Littleport

A young lady from near Littleport
Found fellatio rather fine sport
She was quite the demon
For the taste of semen
And if she could would drink it by the quart

March

The once was a young man from March
Whose dick had a curious arch
Which wasn't so great
Till he made it quite straight
By pressing his manhood with starch

Peterborough

Once in Peterborough out in the Fens
Looking through a telescopic lens
I spied my wife
Fucking the life
Out of a man in a Mercedes Benz

Ramsey*

There once was a lass from Ram-sey
Who scrambled up into a tree
When she got there
Her arse was all bare
And so was her 'see' 'you' 'en' 'tee'

St Ives

An unfortunate chap from St Ives
Learnt the hard way to not play with knives
It was quite a shock
When he chopped off his cock
Which left him feeling somewhat deprived

St Neots

There was a young man from St Ne-ots
Who painted his dick with blue spots
His other pastimes
Were writing stupid rhymes
And collecting his sperm up in pots

Whittlesey

There was a man from Whittle-sey
Whose ball sac it dangled quite free
His balls hung so low
They'd swing to and fro
And whack themselves right on his knee

Wisbech

There was a young man from Wisbech
Who thought his manhood quite a peach
He had a dong
So uncommonly long
The end of it he couldn't reach

Cheshire

Birchwood

A pious young man from Birchwood
Believed self-abuse was not good
But after years of abstention
Close to drawing his pension
He wanked off and came in a flood

Chester*

A young woman got married at Chester
Her mother she kissed and she blessed her
Saying, 'You are in luck
He's a really good fuck
I had him myself down in Leicester'

Congleton

There was a young man from Congle-ton
Whose penis could not be outdone
At a yard long or more
It trailed on the floor
And his bollocks weighed nearly a ton

Crewe*

There once was a whore from Crewe
Who filled her vagina with glue
She said with a grin
They pay to get in
Now they'll pay to get out of it too

Ellesmere Port*

There was a chap from Ellesmere Port
Whose dick was incredibly short
When he climbed into bed
His lady friend said
'That's not a dick it's a wart!'

Frodsham

In Frodsham by the River Weaver
A man was caught by his wife chasing beaver
She said, 'That's the last time
You'll commit that crime'
And castrated him with a meat cleaver

Knutsford

In Knutsford on the Cheshire Plain
Lived a young man with sex on the brain
He never had it as such
But from wanking so much
He had the worst recorded case of wrist strain

Macclesfield

Two young men from Macclesfield
Decided S&M sex appealed
But once a dominatrix
Had stamped on their pricks
They considered their decision repealed

Malpas*

There was an old man from Malpas
Whose bollocks were made out of brass
When jostled together
They played 'Stormy Weather'
And lightning shot from out from his ass

Northwich

An inventor who hailed from Northwich
Made a wanking machine with a glitch
It alas gave his cock
A two forty volt shock
Each time he turned on the switch

Runcorn

There was a young man from Runcorn
Whose routine was the same every morn
He'd shout, 'Tally ho'
Then off he would blow
With a fart like a hunting horn

Sandbach

My love life in the town of Sandbach
Hit quite a nice purple patch
Every woman I met
Seemed quite keen to get
Me on intimate terms with her snatch

Warrington

There was a young man from Warring-ton
Did a fart that just went on and on
An hour after starting
The fart was still farting
Which was when he passed out from the pong

Widnes

At a dogging hotspot in Widnes
I said, 'I know that it's none of my business
But watching you fucking
Was well worth the looking
And I'm pleased to have been a chance witness'

Wilmslow

There was a young man from Wilmslow
Zoophilia attracted him so
And even more queer
He specialised in deer
And buggered three bucks and a doe

Winsford

A hooker from the town of Wins-ford
Had no punters and was feeling bored
But she then walked about
With her tits hanging out
And found she quite easily scored

Cornwall

Bodmin

There was a young man from Bodmin
Whose penis was so long and thin
If he had nothing on
And got a hard-on
His dick would hit him on the chin

Bude

There once was a young man from Bude
Who social conventions eschewed
He said, 'Who cares it's chilly
I'm getting out my willy
Then let's play leapfrog in the nude'

Camborne

There was a lady from Camborne
Who fancied her pubic hair shorn
But she worked on her cunt
With a razor so blunt
The results left her rather forlorn

Falmouth

There once was a whore from Falmouth
Who I must say really did know her stuff
I have to proclaim
I'd already came
Before I even got to near to her muff

Hayle*

On the tits of a barmaid from Hayle
There were tattooed the prices of ale
And on her behind
For the sake of the blind
Was the same information in Braille

Land's End

An unfortunate man from Land's End
Accidentally chopped off his bell end
Being slightly pissed
But a real optimist
He said, 'Do you think it will mend?'

Newquay*

There was a young man from New-quay
Who got stung on the balls by a bee
He made lots of money
By producing pure honey
Each time he attempted to pee

Penzance

A young man who was from Penzance
Thought he'd scored with a lass at a dance
His passion ignited
He got over-excited
And unfortunately came in his pants

Redruth

There once was a whore from Redruth
Who would suck men off in a booth
But business went down
Once word got round
That she had one extremely sharp tooth

St Austell*

There was a young man from St Austell
Who went to a masquerade ball
Just for a stunt
He went dressed as a cunt
And got fucked by a dog in the hall

St Just*

The Right Reverend Dean of St Just
Was gripped by erotical lust
He buggered three men
Two sheep and a hen
And a little green lizard that bust

Truro

There once was a young man from Tru-ro
Whose balls hung particularly low
He wore a jock strap
'Cause otherwise they'd slap
On the floor as they'd swing to and fro

Cumbria

Ambleside

There was a young lady from Ambleside
Whose twat was incredibly wide
If you screwed her all night
You'd be doing alright
If you managed not to fall inside

Barrow-in-Furness*

There once was an old man from Barrow
Who thought he'd try to fuck a sparrow
The sparrow said, 'No
You can't have a go
The hole in my arse is too narrow'

Carlisle

There once was a whore from Carlisle
Who wasn't the most versatile
She said, 'I won't do sucking
And I'll only do fucking
If we stick to the missionary style'

Dalton-in-Furness

A young man from Dalton-in-Furness
At a printers caught his dick in their press
It now looks much flatter
And has printed matter
From the news in the *Daily Express*

Kendal

In the hotel in Kendal I stayed
I was feeling quite down and dismayed
But was slightly less glum
After a quick threesome
With the bellhop and the chambermaid

Keswick*

There was a young lady from Keswick
Who pleasured herself with a stick
Till she got it stuck
And said, 'What the fuck?
Now there's no room in there for a prick'

Kirkby Stephen

A young man from Kirkby Stephen
Had bollocks that were quite uneven
With one very small
The other like a football
If you saw 'em you wouldn't believe 'em

Maryport

There was an old man from Maryport
Whose dick didn't look like it ought
It quite oddly dangled
And the end was all mangled
From the day in his zip it got caught

Millom

I was refused a bank loan in Millom
They said, 'You might masturbate with aplomb
But teaching men how to wank
Is, I'm sorry, to be frank
A business idea that will bomb'

Morecambe Bay

When I was in Morecambe Bay
Something happened that quite made my day
The whore I was screwing
Said, 'I like what you're doing
I'll let you off having to pay'

Penrith

A young lady from Penrith
Was troubled by a unusual whiff
A doctor of acclaim
Thought her twat was to blame
And asked if he might take a sniff

Silloth

A well-to-do man from Silloth
Thought of himself as a toff
He had lots of land
And a house that was grand
And servants paid to wank him off

Whitehaven

A young lady from Whitehaven
Was struck by a rather strange craving
As if in a trance
She pulled down her pants
And pissed all over the paving

Windermere

The deodorant I bought in Windermere
Appeared to have instructions so clear
'Remove cap' it said
'And push up bottom' it read
Now I've got the thing stuck up my rear

Workington

There was a man from Working-ton
Who a shit for four weeks had forgone
Then nature took its course
And expelled with such force
A turd that was seven feet long

Derbyshire

Alfreton

There was a man from Alfre-ton
Who got duped by an internet con
His mail order bride
Was half a mile wide
And instead of a twat had a dong

Belper

There was a young lady from Belper
Who was really a screamer and yelper
Often at night
Her cries of delight
Brought the police by mistake in to help her

Bolsover

There was a young man from Bolsover
Who was pleased with latest legover
Once he'd taken pains
To remove his stains
From the back seat of his dad's Range Rover

Buxton

A TV viewer from Buxton
Thought, 'Flipping heck, now my luck's gone
I've no TV guide
To look inside
So how will I know what the fuck's on'

Chesterfield

A young man from Chesterfield
Found the skin on his dick had all peeled
He sued the nudist camp
For their faulty sun lamp
But I hear that it still hasn't healed

Derby

There was a young lady from Derby city
Had one quite enormous titty
The other alas
Was not in its class
Being quite small which was such a pity

Dronfield

There was an artist from Dronfield
Whose work was a little leftfield
His neighbours were in shock
When a statue of his cock
In thirteen-foot-high granite was revealed

Eckington

I felt my balls for lumps while in Eckington
But I had a slight mishap in checking one
A spasm in my thumb
Meant I over-squeezed one plum
Which I have to say wasn't much fecking fun

Glossop

One day in the town of Glossop
They opened a brand new sex shop
I've bought nothing finer
Than their plastic vagina
But their DVDs weren't that much cop

Heanor

There was a young housewife from Heanor
On sex there was nobody keener
Before a breakfast of toast
She'd had a spit roast
With the milkman and the window cleaner

Ilkeston

Once in the town of Ilkes-ton
There were some very strange goings-on
Involving two vicars
Some old ladies' knickers
And a dildo that was half a yard long

Killamarsh

A young man from near Killamarsh
Had parents who were really harsh
They once caught him wanking
So gave him a spanking
And then dunked his head in the marsh

Long Eaton

I, one day in the town of Long Eaton
Set a record that hasn't been beaten
In a display X-rated
I ejaculated
And my come shot out seventeen feet one

Matlock

There was young man from Matlock
Who had an extraordinary cock
The thing was so long
It fell out his thong
So he'd tuck the end in his sock

Ripley

A daring young couple from Rip-ley
Were having a fuck in a tree
They did not find it frightening
Till they got struck by lightning
A danger they did not foresee

Shirebrook

Stood at a urinal once in Shirebrook
A man said to me, 'Excuse me duck
From where I'm stood
That penis looks good
Could I just take a closer look?'

Staveley

There was a young man from Stave-ley
Whose testicles numbered three
But his extra ball
Did nothing at all
Apart from earn him the nickname ET

Swadlincote

A young lady from Swadlincote
Said, 'I'm not one to boast or to gloat
But with men near and far
I'm most popu-lar
On account of my rather deep throat'

Devon

Ashburton

There was a man I knew from Ashburton
About whom this one thing was certain
If his wife caught him cheating
She'd give him such a beating
That his bollocks for weeks would be hurtin'

Barnstaple

There was a young man from Barn-staple
Who lobbed out his dick on the table
Saying, 'I'm not too fussy
This is for any hussy
As long as she's willing and able'

Bideford*

A Bideford man named Reg
Was screwing this lass in a hedge
When along came his wife
With a big carving knife
And cut off his meat and two veg

Bovey Tracey

A vicar from Bovey Tracey
Wore pants that were frilly and lacy
And at the weekends
In the company of friends
He'd dress up and call himself Stacey

Bradninch

A doctor who hailed from Bradninch
Said, 'This circumcision lark is a cinch
I once was so bold
As to do it blindfold
And just chopped off the odd extra inch'

Brixham

A photographers' model from Brixham
Had a chest that would truly transfix 'em
They would all take snaps
Of her lovely baps
And long to get their dicks in betwixt 'em

Buckfastleigh

A young lady from Buckfast-leigh
Filled up her twat with pot-pourri
It was a pleasing smell
But fucking her was hell
On account of the floral debris

Dawlish

I met a mermaid from Dawlish
To screw her was my dearest wish
But I hadn't a clue
What exactly to do
On account of her being half fish

Exeter[*]

There was a young lady from Exeter
So lovely that men craned their necks at her
But one chap depraved
Disgustingly waved
The distinguishing part of his sex at her

Exmouth

In Exmouth on the River Exe
I was asked to join in some group sex
But at the sight of such sin
Before I could join in
I prematurely came in my kecks

Ilfracombe

A young lady from Ilfracombe
Liked to pleasure herself with a broom
She thought the handle was great
With which to masturbate
And at the same time she could sweep the room

Ivybridge

A young lady from Ivybridge
Kept a dildo in her fridge
She said, 'Hell, why not?
If I'm feeling hot
It cools me right down in a smidge'

Newton Abbot

There was a young lady from Newton Abbot
Who sought sex wheree'er she could grab it
But each year for Lent
The men she forwent
And just stuck with her Rampant Rabbit

Ottery St Mary

There was a maid from Ottery St Mary
Whose body was incredibly hairy
'She must be a man'
Said my friend Stan
But I found her twat and proved the contrary

Paignton

There was a young man from Paign-ton
Had an accident with his airgun
It went off in his pocket
And with a nasty shock, it
Brought his bollocks in number to one

Plymouth

An old man from Plymouth in Devon
Thought he'd died and gone to heaven
He ordered one whore
But they sent on six more
And he ended up fucking all seven

Tavistock

There was a young man from Tavistock
Who had a most extraordinary cock
On the hour to perfection
It twitched with erection
Like the cuckoo in his favourite clock

Tiverton

In the Devon town of Tiver-ton
I was chatting to the most charming nun
When it was enough iffy
For me to get a stiffy
Let alone I'd left my flies undone

Torquay

There was a young lady from Torquay
Who went on a mad fucking spree
She first screwed a teacher
A cook, then a preacher
Then Torquay United FC

Dorset

Blandford Forum

There were two sisters from Blandford Forum
And one time there I did implore 'em
To both come to bed
And both give me head
Which they did, you just got to adore 'em

Bournemouth

A nudist from Bournemouth Pavilion
Admitted to being a silly 'un
When he caught his pubic hair
Folding up a deck chair
And gave himself a makeshift Brazilian

Bridport

There was a young man from Bridport
Who was having a wank and got caught
His quick five knuckle shuffle
Caused quite a kerfuffle
As it was done on public transport

Christchurch

There was a student from Christchurch
Who did some peculiar research
He studied pain
To no particular gain
By whacking his balls with a birch

Dorchester

One day a vicar from Dorchester
Bought a nightie made from polyester
Next came pink slacks
Skirts and sling-backs
Till he insisted his friends call him Esther

Ferndown

The young lady I met from Ferndown
Was my cheapest date ever, hands down
She paid for lunch at Tesco
Then we screwed al fresco
And she tipped me with two or three pounds

Lyme Regis

There once was a young man from Lyme
Who found his cock covered with grime
But it was quite dras-tic
For him to clean his dick
With scouring pads and caustic lime

Poole*

There was a young lover from Poole
Felt his ardour grow suddenly cool
No lack of affection
Reduced his erection
But his zipper had just caught his tool

Portland

There was a young lady from Portland
Said to her man, 'Our sex is grand
Your cock is a peach
But must we fuck on the beach?
My twat is now filled up with sand!'

Purbeck

There was an old man from Pur-beck
Who wrapped both his feet round his neck
In this position
It was his disposition
To suck himself off in a sec

Swanage

On a beach on the Swanage coast
I saw a sight that had me engrossed
A lass took out her baps
Then invited two chaps
To indulge themselves in a spit roast

Tolpuddle*

In Tolpuddle there once was a martyr
Who was an incredible farter
On the strength of one bean
He'd play 'God Save the Queen'
And Beethoven's 'Moonlight Sonata'

Verwood

There was a young man from Verwood
Who fashioned a cunt out of wood
But regretted his home-made
Masturbation aid
When a splinter stuck in his manhood

Weymouth

A dominatrix from Weymouth Pavilion
Proclaimed I was one in a million
When I didn't mind
When she whipped my behind
Till my bum was a shade of vermilion

Wimborne Minster

To a young lady from Wimborne Minster
I said, 'I'm sorry you think that I minced there
My curious gait
Is 'cause my pants aren't quite straight'
But I don't think that really convinced her

Durham

Billingham

A trick of this young man from Billingham
Amused all his friends, quite thrilling 'em
To an incredible cheer
He'd balance two pints of beer
On the end of his cock without spilling 'em

Bishop Auckland

There was a young man from Bishop Auck-land
Whose job interview did not go as planned
The panel of selection
Gave him a stray erection
And his hopes of success turned to sand

Chester-le-Street

There was a man from Chester-le-Street
Who achieved a magnificent feat
Using tackle and block
Attached to his cock
He lifted half a ton of concrete

Consett

There was a young man from Con-sett
Who was rather too fond of his pet
It seems it's illegal
To fuck one's own beagle
And his crime was found out by the vet

Crook

There once was a young man from Crook
Whose dick was shaped just like a hook
It was no good for shagging
'Cause it just kept on snagging
But for fishing he was really in luck

Darlington

There was a young man from Darling-ton
Who had quite an incredible dong
When it was hard
It measured near on a yard
Which you've got to admit is quite long

Durham

There was an old man from Durham
Who was feeling particularly glum
He'd been wanking away
For over a day
And still hadn't managed to come

Ferryhill[*]

A young lady from Ferryhill
Fucked a dynamite stick for a thrill
They found her vagina
In North Carolina
And bits of her tits in Brazil

Hartlepool

There was a young man from Hartlepool
Who had a magnificent tool
He had a shlong
That was twelve inches long
But he wouldn't use it as a rule

Newton Aycliffe

A contortionist from Newton Aycliffe
Could give his own arsehole a sniff
But he once got a start
When he let go a fart
And damn near passed out from the whiff

Peterlee

There was a young man from Peterlee
Who swung by his dick from a tree
It stretched like elastic
Then shot back quite drastic
And he wailed like a screaming banshee

Seaham

There was a young man from Sea-ham
Who broke wind whenever he swam
His farts were so strong
They propelled him along
With the force of a battering ram

Spennymoor*

There was a young man from Spennymoor
Whose tool was a yard long or more
So he wore the thing
In a surgical sling
To stop it from wiping the floor

Stanley

There once was a young man from Stanley
Who was feeling exceptionally randy
When in walked a hooker
Who was quite a looker
He said, 'Fuck me, that's really quite handy'

Stockton-on-Tees*

A young man from Stockton-on-Tees
Was stung on his dick by some bees
He said in surprise
As his dick grew in size
'They can do it again if they please'

East Sussex

Battle

A farmer and his lassie from Battle
Were fucking, when the farmer said, 'That'll
Just have to do
I'll have to stop mid-screw
'Cause it's time for me to feed the cattle'

Bexhill-on-Sea

There was a lass from Bexhill-on-Sea
Who was feeling young and fancy free
But with no conception
Of any contraception
She soon had a baby or three

Brighton*

There was a young fellow from Brighton
Who said to his girl, 'You've a tight one'
She said, 'Pardon my soul
But you're in the wrong hole
There's plenty of room in the right one'

Crowborough

To a dominatrix from Crow-borough
I said, 'I faced you at first with such horror
But you handle femdom
With so much aplomb
Can I come back for some more tomorrer?'

Eastbourne*

There was a young man from Eastbourne
Who wished that he'd never been born
And he wouldn't have been
If his father had seen
That the end of his rubber was torn

Hailsham

To this lady at the Hailsham Museum
Said I with thoughts to 'carpe diem'
'I've two nice round artefacts
That I keep in my slacks'
And I got them out for her to see 'em

Hastings

There was a young lady from Has-tings
Whose twat could do amazing things
In a sight quite bizarre
It'd smoke a cigar
And blow the most perfect smoke rings

Hove

There once was an old man from Hove
Who his wife to distraction he drove
Till one day she flipped
And off his balls clipped
Then boiled them in brine on the stove

Lewes

A careless young man from Lewes
Would never look where he would piss
To give him his dues
He rarely wet his shoes
But his trousers were more hit and miss

Newhaven

To the young lady I met in Newhaven
I said, 'Don't you think it's rather brazen
To give me hand relief
Whilst we're on a public beach
At a speed that might cause me abrasion?'

Polegate

The young lady I met in Polegate
I found to be a bit too sedate
She'd only let me pet her
Outside her sweater
And that on our ninety-sixth date

Rye

There once was an old man from Rye
Whose home was just like a pig sty
It was overrun with rats
And the loft it had bats
That pissed in his water supply

Seaford

At a bus stop one day in Sea-ford[†]
A young lady said to me, 'I'm bored
I know we're in the street
But if I'm discrete
Could I have a play with your pork sword?'

Uckfield

If you go to the town of Uckfield
And want to see sex unconcealed
There are lots and lots
Of dogging hot spots
So be sure to keep your eyes peeled

[†] The traditional Sussex pronunciation of Seaford does actually have a full vowel in each syllable: 'Sea-ford'.

East Yorkshire

Beverley

There once was a chemist from Beverley
Who made potions, he thought, most cleverly
But one had a side effect
That he didn't expect
That made his dick the smallest you'd ever see

Bridlington

There once was a young man from Bridlington
Who was not getting very much diddling done
He said to his chick
'Don't you like my dick?
It is at least a fair to middling one'

Brough

At a job interview I had in Brough[†]
They said, 'Really, enough is enough
We could turn a blind eye
To you not wearing a tie
But why have come in the buff?'

[†] Pronounced 'Bruff'

Driffield

Out on the Driffield Navigation[‡]
A young lady and I had relations
But the rocking of the barge
Speeded up my discharge
And she was unimpressed with my duration

Goole*

There once was a young man from Goole
Who found little red spots on his tool
His doctor a cynic
Said, 'Get out of my clinic
And wipe off that lipstick you fool!'

Hornsea

There once was a lass from Hornsea
Who said, 'I'll invite round for tea
Every man that I've fucked
Or even just sucked
Damn it, I'm going to need a marquee'

Hull

Said a husband to his wife from Hull
'I know we don't want our sex to be dull
But I think we could add spice
Without the need for the mice
Those chickens, the goats or that bull'

[‡] The canal in the town

Pocklington

A young man from Pockling-ton
Had farts that just went on and on
To share this gift
He would find a crowded lift
And let all inside share the pong

Snaith

When I was at the library in Snaith
I found my trousers starting to chafe
So to looks of disapproval
I made with their removal
And my underpants too to be safe

South Cave*

There was an old man from South Cave
Who dug up a whore from a grave
Though she was rotting like shit
And had only one tit
He said, 'Think of the money I'll save'

Withernsea

If you're after a day of fun and frolics
Without drug dealers or alcoholics
To spend the day through
With plenty to do
Don't go to Withernsea 'cause it's bollocks

Essex

Basildon

A body builder from Basil-don
Thought his dick might be really quite strong
He tried without luck
To use it to pull a truck
But was pleased to see that made it quite long

Billericay

One day a mother from Billericay
Found her Ann Summers catalogue sticky
She said to her son
'What have you done?
Have you wanked over this again, Ricky?'

Braintree

There was a young man from Braintree
Who ate asparagus from breakfast till tea
Not for the flavour
Which he didn't savour
But for the smell that it gave to his pee

Brentwood

A lady vampire from Brentwood
At vampiring was not very good
But every four weeks
You might hear her shrieks
As she drank down her own menstrual blood

Burnham-on-Crouch

A young man from Burnham-on-Crouch
Was trying to screw a whore on a couch
When she said to him
'You've not found my quim
You've been fucking my tobacco pouch'

Canvey Island

There was a young man from Canvey Is-land
Whose wedding night did not go as planned
He found his new wife
Fucking the life
Out of the Aveley and Newham Brass Band

Chelmsford

A young man from Chelmsford, Essex
Took steroids with adverse effects
So many anabolics
Had so shrunk his bollocks
To see them he needed his specs

Chigwell

Whilst fucking this lass in Chigwell
Something happened I couldn't foretell
Her mother walked in
And said with a grin
'Do you mind if I join in as well?'

Chipping Ongar

There was a man from Chipping Ongar
Who had an incredible donger
Wherever you'd roam
This side of John Holmes
You'd not find a dick that was longer

Clacton-on-Sea

A young man from Clacton-on-Sea
Said, 'Just look how far I can pee
I'm hard to beat
Never mind twenty feet
I can piss right from here to Braintree!'

Colchester

There was a young lady from Colchester
And her ex she did constantly pester
She made constant phone calls
Then chopped off his balls
And this led the police to arrest her

Grays

There was a sex worker from Grays
Who was rather impressed with my ways
When we'd finished screwing
I said, 'What're you doing?
It's supposed to be me that pays'

Hadleigh

There was a young lady from Hadleigh
Who wanted to make love to me madly
Which excited me so
That at the word 'go'
I came in my pants, rather sadly

Harlow

A young lady from Harlow
Wore shorts that were really tight so
She made sure you saw her
Labia majora
In outline, with her camel toe

Harwich

There was a young man from Harwich
With an unnatural love of cross-stitch
To see such needlework
Would drive him berserk
And his penis would violently twitch

Leigh-on-Sea*

There was a young plumber from Leigh
Who was plumbing a lass by the sea
When she said, 'Someone's coming'
He replied (while still plumbing)
'If anyone's coming it's me!'

Loughton

A novice nun from Loughton†
Said, 'Truly I am a devout 'un
I'm forsaking all boys
And just stick with sex toys
In fact I am never without one'

Pitsea

There was a fellow from Pitsea
Caught by his wife in flagrante
This made her so mad
She chopped off his 'nads
And hung them from the Christmas tree

Rayleigh

There once was a young man from Rayleigh
Who ended up at the Old Bailey
For exposing his parts
In the shopping mart
And doing so nineteen times daily

---

† Pronounced 'Lout-un'

Saffron Walden

A young lady from Saffron Walden
Was surely a sight worth beholdin'
But you'd have been conned
If you thought her real blonde
Her pubes were dark brown and not golden

Shoeburyness

A young man from Shoeburyness
Caught his penis once in a punch press
Perforating his winkie
Which made it quite sprinkly
So when pissing he made quite a mess

Southend-on-Sea

A young man from Southend-on-Sea
Had a crap from the top of a tree
Which landed in the lap
Of an irritated chap
Who said, 'I will fucking kill thee'

South Woodham Ferrers

A 'brit milah' in South Woodham Ferrers
Turned into a day of sheer terror
Alas the circumcisist
Had got himself pissed
And sliced off the boy's cock in error

Stanford-le-Hope

At the B&B at Stanford-le-Hope
I was down and inclined to just mope
But my mood was revised
When the landlady surprised
Me with the offer of a tit-wank with soap

Tilbury

One day at the Tilbury docks
I stripped off in a telephone box
My original plan
Was to be Superman
But I came out just wearing my socks

Waltham Abbey

A young lady from Waltham Abbey
Had manners I thought a bit shabby
She arrived for our date
About half an hour late
And explained she'd been fucking the cabbie

Walton-on-the-Naze

A young man from Walton-on-the-Naze
Said, 'I'll put on a show to amaze
Find me a hussy
Who's not very fussy
And I'll fuck her in sixty-nine ways'

Wickford

A young man from Wickford, Es-sex
Took steroids to tone up his pecs
But he wasn't so pleased
To see his testes
Had shrunk to two tiny objects

Witham

There once was a young man from Witham
Who'd eat just whatever you'd give 'im
It would not turn his guts
To eat a bull's nuts
And its penis to go along with 'em

Gloucestershire

Bradley Stoke

There was a lady from Bradley Stoke
With whom I was enjoying a poke
When her husband walked in
And punched me on the chin
Which put me a bit off my stroke

Cheltenham

I tried wearing tights when in Cheltenham
To see for a change how I felt in 'em
But my crotch got so hot
I thought, 'Perhaps not'
For fear that my bollocks might melt in 'em

Cirencester

A young lady from Cirencester
Had a job as a vibrator tester
But what drove her berserk
After years of such work
Was she couldn't find a dick that impressed her

Filton

There once was a young man from Filton
With a problem when he put a kilt on
His knob cheese would entice
All the neighbourhood mice
To run up his legs for his stilton

Gloucester

Drink ruined the hope I did foster
When I seduced this young lady from Gloucester
After forty Captain Morgans
My sexual organs
Were in no fit state to accost her

Lechlade

There was a young man from Lechlade
Who once sat on a hand grenade
He got quite a shock
Lost his balls and his cock
And was left feeling somewhat dismayed

Lydney*

There was a young lady from Lydney
Who could take it right up to the kidney
But a man from Quebec
Put it up to her neck
My, he had a long one now, didn't he?

Northleach

There was a lady from Northleach
Who sexual positions would teach
For a joint booking
On her course in fucking
She'd only charge fifteen pounds each

Stonehouse

There was a young lady from Stonehouse
With one rather large pubic louse
She kept it well fed
On fanny batter and bread
Till it was roughly the size of a mouse

Stow-on-the-Wold

There was a man from Stow-on-the-Wold
Whose dick was all covered with mould
He said, 'No one goes there
But I find the green fur
Prevents me from feeling the cold'

Stroud

There once was a young man from Stroud
Whose farts were incredibly loud
At ten decibels
And with quite awful smells
They could quickly disperse any crowd

Tewkesbury

There was a young man from Tewkes-bury
Who would only eat vindaloo curry
His stools were so soft
That whenever he coughed
He would fill up his pants in a hurry

Thornbury

There was a young man from Thorn-bury
Who would only eat vindaloo curry
His farts you could bet
Were incredibly wet
And would empty the room in a hurry

Wickwar

There was a young man from Wickwar
Whose wrists were both feeling quite sore
He said, 'I wasn't banking
On quite that much wanking
And my penis is nearly red raw'

Wotton-under-Edge

There was a young lady from Wotton
Who became a bit of a glutton
Her arse got so fat
When she sat down to crap
She could barely get half off her butt on

Yate

There was a young man from Yate
Whose penis so was far from straight
Its ninety degree bend
Meant that sex would depend
On him finding the strangest bedmate

Greater London

Barking

There once was a young man from Barking
Who on risky things was often embarking
He'd a curious trait
To use his dick as bait
When he went out sea-fishing or sharking

Barnet

A young lady from Barnet Fair
Had incredibly long pubic hair
There'd be no surviving
If you went muff-diving
Some hundreds had got lost in there

Bexley

Once in Bexley on the River Cray
I went to a wife-swapping soiree
But frankly my swap
Just wasn't much cop
What with her moustache and toupee

Brent*

There once was a young man from Brent
Whose dick was incredibly bent
The curve was such trouble
He folded it double
So instead of coming he went

Bromley

There once was a vicar from Bromley
Whose behaviour was quite an anomaly
In the strange circumstance
When he pulled down his pants
In the middle of giving a homily†

Camden

There once tried a couple from Camden
To have sex whilst riding their tandem
And on Old Compton Street
They achieved the feat
So kudos you do have to hand 'em

Chelsea

There was a young man from Chelsea
Who covered his penis with brie
Saying, 'My girl will savour
That cheesy French flavour
When served with a glass of Chablis'

---

† A sermon that follows the reading of a scripture, in case a definition
is required

Croydon

A factory making sex toys in Croydon
Had an opening that might suit a hoyden[‡]
Subject to a test
Of her technique and her zest
Dildo-testing she might be employed on

Dagenham

There was a young lady from Dagenham
Who was tired on her feet and was dragging 'em
Two men made her a gift
Of a homeward bound lift
And she thanked them both kindly by shagging 'em

Ealing[*]

There was a young lady from Ealing
Who had a peculiar feeling
She lay on her back
And opened her crack
And pissed all over the ceiling

Enfield

There was a young man from Enfield
Who said, 'Look at the penis I wield
Its girth, length and weight
Are all very great
It's a winner in every field'

[‡] A somewhat archaic term for a boisterous young woman (Not a lot rhymes with Croydon!)

Fulham

A masochist who hailed from Ful-ham
Held his dick out against a door jamb
Saying, 'If you don't mind
Would you be so kind
As to give this here door a big slam?'

Greenwich

There was a young man from Greenwich
Who was cast on a spell by a witch
Which made his dong
So unreasonably long
He kept it tied in a half-hitch

Hackney

As a chemist I worked once in Hackney
And invented a treatment for acne
But one ingredi-ent
Was semen I'd spent
And they thought that good reason to sack me

Hammersmith

One night at the Hammersmith Palais[††]
I met a lass with breast implants called Sally
And was thrilled to bits
To get my dick between her tits
As she let me fuck her Silicon Valley

[††] Obviously this was before it was demolished in 2012.

Haringey

A young lady from Haringey
Ate nothing but beans for a day
Her farts of such size
Were no real surprise
Her shock was their fragrant bouquet

Harrow*

There once was a young man from Harrow
Whose knob was the size of a marrow
He said to a tart
'Try this for a start
My balls are outside on a barrow'

Havering

There was a young lady from Havering
Whose devotion to dick was unwavering
By noon she had drunk
A pint's worth of spunk
All sucked from the cocks she'd been savouring

Hillingdon

I caught some virulent crabs in Hillingdon
(After a night I will say was thrilling fun)
After treatment with lotions
And various potions
I don't think I succeeded in killing one

Hounslow

There was a young man from Hounslow
Whose dick was shaped just like a hoe
He used it in the garden
When he had a hard-on
For planting his flowers in a row

Islington*

A young man from Islington Green
Invented a wanking machine
On the ninety-ninth stroke
The fucking thing broke
And whipped up his balls to a cream

Kensington

This lazy chap from Kensing-ton
Would never get anything done
Even using toilet tissue
Was a bit of an issue
So he was often left with a Klingon

Kingston upon Thames

A young man from Kingston on Thames
Thought, 'I must give my penis a cleanse'
He gave it a good clean
With some Mr Sheen
And showed the results to his friends

Lewisham

At this sex shop in Lewi-sham
I complained their products were a sham:
'I wanted a finely made
Masturbation aid
And you've sold me a hollowed out yam'

Mayfair

Prayed he, a bishop from Mayfair
'Give me stiffness and strength not despair'
When on self-inspection
He found he'd an erection
And said 'Lord, you have answered my prayer'

Merton

I once knew a young lady from Merton
But I know I upset her for certain
For when we'd finished fucking
I thought she wasn't looking
When I wiped off my dick on the curtain

Newham

There once was an artist from Newham
Who took out his bollocks and drew 'em
After some sketchings
He created some etchings
And charged twenty pounds just to view 'em

Redbridge

There was a young man from Redbridge
Who got himself locked in a fridge
By the time it was night
His dick had frostbite
And his bollocks had shrunk by a smidge

Richmond upon Thames

There once was a whore from Richmond
Who I found so extremely rotund
That in amongst her fat
I just couldn't find a twat
So I asked, 'Could I have a refund?'

Southall*

There was a young man from Southall
Who swore he had only one ball
But two little bitches
Unbuttoned his britches
And found he had no balls at all

Sutton

There once was a young man from Sutton
Who manure on his cock he did put on
He'd been told it would grow
If he treated it so
He wasn't as bright as a button

Tooting

There once was a young man from Tooting
Who'd expose himself when commuting
Till one fateful day
Much to his dismay
A lass gave his balls a good booting

Walthamstow

There was a young lady from Walthamstow
Whose labia hung a little bit low
She had one or two mishaps
With her over-long piss-flaps
Till she tied them up into a bow

Wapping

There once was a young man from Wapping
Set a record that will take some topping
One night in no hurry
After quite a large curry
He broke wind for an hour without stopping

Waterloo

There was a young man from Waterloo
With a business idea to pursue
To bottle his spunk
For sale to be drunk
Or be used as organic shampoo

Greater Manchester

Altrincham

There was a young man from Altrincham
Who ate only tin, spice and ham
Though this dietary fad
Was really quite mad
He found he could shit cans of Spam

Ashton-under-Lyne

A butcher from Ashton-under-Lyne
Would not waste one bit of dead swine
He'd save up pigs' ears
For years and for years
And pickle their bollocks in brine

Bolton

In Bolton town in the North West
They once held a pissing contest
But the judges were biased
I did piss the highest
I just think they liked my penis less

Bramhall

An unfortunate man from Bramhall
On some broken glass once had a fall
It gave him a shock
To lose half his cock
And be left with only one ball

Bury

There once was a young man from Bury
Who one night was set to lose his cherry
Dutch courage he'd sought
But his knob would do naught
After he'd had two bottles of sherry

Cheadle

To his girlfriend a young man from Cheadle
Said, 'I'm sorry my erection's so feeble
It was alright last night
When I turned out the light
And snuggled up with my pet beagle'

Denton

There once was a young man from Denton
Who had an exceptionally bent 'un
He tried hard to create
A machine to make it straight
But try as he might couldn't invent one

Eccles

In Eccles they have these strange cakes
That give me the worst stomach aches
One case of diarrhoea
Was so fucking severe
It left me for weeks with the shakes

Golborne

There was an old man from Golborne
Who spent all his time most forlorn
Till he found a new hobby
Which enlivened his knob, he
Spent all of his time watching porn

Heywood

There was a young lady from Heywood
Whose twat didn't look like it should
Her piss-flaps were longer
Than the average donger
And dwarfed by her clitoral hood

Hyde

There was a young lady from Hyde
Who wore her new bikini bottoms with pride
Until her friend Kim
Said, 'Your bush needs a trim
Look at those spiders' legs out the side'

Leigh*

A young lady from Leigh was at sea
And she said, 'How it hurts me to pee'
'I see,' said the mate
'That accounts for the state
Of the purser, the captain and me'

Manchester

There was a young man from Manchester
Who brought home a nice girl and undressed her
But she came over queasy
'Cause his knob was so cheesy
It resembled a piece of Red Leicester

Middleton

There was a young lady from Middleton
Who would take out a nipple and twiddle one
Saying, 'What makes me blue
Is I've only got two
I'd love to have an extra middle one'

Oldham

There was a young man from Oldham
Who lost big playing Texas Hold 'Em
To pay the all the debt
From his last losing bet
He chopped off his bollocks and sold 'em

Prestwich

There once was a man from Prestwich
Who was so very idle and rich
He employed a factotum
Just to scratch his scrotum
In case his balls would have an itch

Radcliffe

There was a young man from Radcliffe
Who felt strange after smoking a spliff
He started to feel
A dog would appeal
And set off to seduce his mastiff

Ramsbottom

There was a young man from Ramsbottom
Who said, 'Pubic lice I have got 'em
But when they move about
I will pick 'em out
And put 'em on the table and swat 'em'

Rochdale

There was a young man from Rochdale
Whose farts were quite beyond the pale
From his arse they'd propel
With an outrageous smell
And a force off the Beaufort scale

Sale

There once was a young man from Sale
Who tried to make love to a whale
But with the size of its quim
All he did was fall in
And thought, 'Next time I'll try a sea snail'

Salford

A young man from Salford Quays
Once locked himself in a deep freeze
In almost a trice
His dick was like ice
And his balls shrivelled up like dried peas

Stockport

There was a young man from Stockport
With the world's biggest penile wart
It was a nightmare
And it required its own fare
When he travelled on public transport

Stretford

In Stretford the home of United
Lived a young man who was so short-sighted
He mixed up his girl's mott
With the hole in her bott
But happily she was delighted

Swinton

The T-shirt I ordered from Swinton
Came with a little misprint on
Instead of 'I ♥ ROCK'
It read 'I ♥ COCK'
Not exactly what I was intent on

Tyldesley

There was a young lady from Tyldes-ley
Who was so keen on daytime TV
She'd be glued to the screen
Flicking her bean
From nine till at least half past three

Urmston

There was a young man from Urms-ton
With a dick big as a Bofors gun
He said, 'It's a curse
And you know what is worse
My bollocks weigh nearly a ton!'

Wigan

There was a young man from Wigan
Who didn't have much of a big 'un
At the swimming baths
He would pass for a lass
With a bikini top and a wig on

Hampshire

Aldershot

There was a young man from Aldershot
Who on anatomy wasn't so hot
He couldn't tell tits
From a lady's other bits
Or a clitoris from a G-spot

Andover

I once met a lass from Andover
And we went for a roll in the clover
Which she thought was so nice
That after doing it twice
She said, 'Can we do it nineteen times over?'

Basingstoke

There was a young man from Basingstoke
Who was quite an extraordinary bloke
He'd get out his dick
And whack it with a brick
Which was not a thing enjoyed by most folk

Eastleigh

There once was a young man from Eastleigh
Who had habits quite strange and most beastly
He'd fart in a crowd
Whilst reading aloud
Some passages from J.B.Priestley

Fareham

There once was a young man from Fareham
Who'd buy ladies' panties and wear 'em
When his wife found out
She gave him a clout
Till he said, 'Very well, I will share 'em'

Farnborough

In Farnborough they have an airshow
Where I offered to put on a show
Of naked hang-gliding
But they were quick at deciding
The answer was definitely 'no'

Fleet

There once was a farmer from Fleet
Who thought that his sheep looked a treat
He took out his cock
And had fucked the whole flock
By lunchtime, which was quite a feat

Gosport

There was a head chef from Gosport
Who was feeling a bit overwrought
It was quite fundamental
That he had gone mental
When he stuck his dick in the fruit torte

Havant

There was a young man from Havant
Whose regard for his flatmate was scant
He'd make noise and mess
Just to cause him distress
And then piss in his best spider plant

Portsmouth

There once was a young man from Pompey†
Whose face was quite ugly and wonky
His girlfriend, a cutie
Saw in him no beauty
But she said he was hung like a donkey

Southampton

There was a young man from Southampton
Who always had nipple clamps clamped on
And who liked nothing more
Than being chained to the floor
And having his bollocks quite stamped on

---

† A nickname for the city of Portsmouth as well as its football club

Winchester

Legend tells of a man from Winchester
Whose bollocks had started to fester
Till he had a big cough
And his balls flew right off
And landed in the outskirts of Leicester

Herefordshire

Bromyard

There was a young man from Bromyard
Whose evening was terribly marred
He burnt his private parts
When setting light to his farts
Leaving his bollocks quite charred

Hereford

In Hereford on the River Wye
In a tea shop I once did come by
The proprietress, good looking
Was no good at cooking
But I can recommend her hair pie

Ledbury

An adventurous chef from Ledbury
Served dishes that were sometimes a worry
His favourite main course
Was the dick from a horse
With its bollocks served up in a curry

Leominster

In Leominster, a name some mispronounce
I marched through the streets with a flounce
This strange manner of walking
Set some people talking
But I liked the way it made my balls bounce

Ross-on-Wye

A young fellow from Ross-on-Wye
Explained his plans had gone awry:
'I'm afraid you must pardon
My permanent hard-on
I've taken too much Spanish fly'

Hertfordshire

Baldock

There was a young man from Baldock
Who had an extraordinary cock
In its tumidity
It was of such rigidity
He could use it for drilling rock

Berkhamsted

There was a man from Berkhamsted
Who once fucked a fresh loaf of bread
He was heard to utter
'It'd be better with butter
Or even some margarine spread'

Bishop's Stortford

In the town of Bishop's Stortford, Herts
Lived a young man with incredible farts
When he let them loose
Such tunes he'd produce
He won a master's in musical arts

Borehamwood

There was a young man from Borehamwood
Whose dick didn't look like it should
It its flaccid state
It looked fairly straight
But it was ninety degrees when it stood

Bushey

A pubic louse on a chap from Bushey
Said to its pals, 'Do not think me pushy
But I'm going to transfer
To his girlfriend's pubic hair
On account of it being more bushy

Cheshunt*

There was a young man from Cheshunt
Whose cock did a marvellous stunt
His versatile spout
Could be turned inside out
And thereafter be used as a cunt

Harpenden

There was a young man from Harpenden, Herts
With the most enormous private parts
He needed tackle and block
Just to lift his cock
And for his balls he used two shopping carts

Hatfield

A Scotsman went to church in Hatfield
But broke wind as to pray he kneeled
And to add to his guilt
The blast raised his kilt
And left him with his bare arse revealed

Hemel Hempstead

A young lady from Hemel Hempstead
Liked to spank me with a stale French bread
After three afternoons
My arse was like a baboon's
Being coloured a purplish red

Hertford

At the Hertford Corn Exchange
I met a whore pleasantly strange
She had no aversion
To any perversion
And her price was just a bit of small change

Hitchin*

There was a young lady from Hitchin
Who was scratching her crotch in the kitchen
Her mother said, 'Rose,
It's crabs I suppose'
She said, 'Bollocks, get on with your knitting'

Letchworth

Said a young man who hailed from Letchworth:
'I must have the biggest dick on earth
It's possible your donger
Is slightly longer
But mine makes up for it with the girth'

Potters Bar

There was a maestro from Potter's Bar
Whose passion for his art went too far
The violin section
Would give him an erection
When conducting the orches-tra

Rickmansworth

There once was a young man from Ricky
Who found having sex very tricky
Alas his love spuds
Were a right pair of duds
And the same could be said of his dicky

St Albans

A young lady from St Al-bans
Had a really large number of fans
Not 'cause she could sing
Or in fact do a thing
But on account of her mammary glands

Stevenage*

A Stevenage man named Reg
Was screwing this lass in a hedge
When along came his wife
With a big carving knife
And cut off his meat and two veg

Tring

There was a young lady from Tring
Who could do an incredible thing
If she ate all the time
Juniper berries and lime
She could piss out a perfect gin sling

Waltham Cross

A young man from near Waltham Cross
Would eight times a day have a toss
It was his inclination
To turn to masturbation
Whenever he was at a loss

Ware

There was a young lady from Ware
Whose body was covered in hair
If she wanted a fucking
You'd spend all day looking
For a twat that was somewhere in there

Welwyn Garden City

This limerick for Welwyn Garden City
Was written for me by committee
So it scans even worse than some of mine
It might just about rhyme
But it's certainly not dirty or witty

Isle of Wight

Brading

There was a young lady from Brading
Who I was at the time serenading
I sang her a song
About the size of my dong
Then she didn't take too much persuading

Cowes

I was once in a book shop in Cowes
But alas had to leave in mid-browse
I had been looking
At a book about fucking
And it was noticed my dick had aroused

Freshwater

At an inn in the town of Freshwater
I was enjoying a nice pint of porter
When the obliging landlord
Said that if I was bored
If I wanted I could fuck his daughter

Godshill*

There was a young man from Godshill
Who ate dynamite for a thrill
His navel corroded
His arsehole exploded
And they found both his nuts in Brazil

Lake

There was a young fellow from Lake
Whose large organ was actually fake
It looked quite impressive
If a fraction excessive
But fell off if he gave it a shake

Newport*

A lawyer from Newport, Isle of Wight
Couldn't fuck 'cause her twat was too tight
She discovered a loophole
By using her poophole
And now she fucks all day and night

Ryde

There was a young lady from Ryde
With a twat that was really quiet wide
She'd put in her finger
But it wouldn't long linger
Before half her arm was inside

Sandown

There was a young man from Sandown
Whose expression turned into a frown
He came home to find his dad
Had gone slightly mad
And was wanking whilst dressed as a clown

Shanklin

A chap from Shanklin esplanade
Once scored with a lovely mermaid
She was quite a dish
But with her being half fish
The problem was how to get laid

Ventnor

I found in the town of Vent-nor
A porn stash in a bric-a-brac store
But it took me a while
To go through the pile
Till I found something halfway hardcore

Kent

Ashford

There was a young man from Ashford, Kent
Who once gave up wanking for Lent
Forty days later
A reborn masturbator
He sperm was like rubber cement

Broadstairs

There was a young lady from Broadstairs
With exceedingly long pubic hairs
She never thought to trim
The hairs on her quim
Till she tripped on them climbing the stairs

Canterbury

Canterbury's known for its tales
And the lass that this poem details
To be somewhat blunt
Had a rather large cunt
That was roughly the size of a whale's

Chatham

Once in Chatham in the Medway
I spent an incredible day
In the arms of a whore
Who fucked me quite sore
And forgot to ask me to pay

Dartford

There was a young man from Dartford, Kent
Who once gave up wanking for Lent
Afterwards he released
From his pole lightly greased
His sperm in a raging torrent

Deal*

There was a young lady from Deal
Who once had sex with an eel
One morning at dawn
She gave birth to a prawn
Two crabs and a small baby seal

Dover

Once in Dover with its cliffs of white
Lived a young man who wasn't that bright
He brushed his teeth to a sheen
With haemorrhoid cream
And put toothpaste on his arsehole at night

Folkestone

There was an old man from Folk-stone
Who most often would be found alone
He lived in a cave
And never did bathe
But instead soaked his balls in cologne

Gillingham

I met two young ladies from Gillingham
And had hopes in the sack to be thrilling 'em
But such was their allure
I came premature
After less than two minutes of drilling 'em

Gravesend

There was a young man from Gravesend
Whose dick had a curious bend
But it worried him not
And 'cause it hit her G-spot
It was a hit with his girlfriend

Herne Bay*

There was a young man from Herne Bay
Who fashioned a cunt out of clay
But the heat of his dick
Turned the clay into brick
And chafed all his foreskin away

Hythe

There once was a young man from Hythe
Who had an overactive sex drive
Sick of having to pardon
His permanent hard-on
He chopped off his balls with a scythe

Lydd

There once was a young man from Lydd
Who tried to make love to a squid
Little did he think
He'd get covered in ink
And wish he hadn't done what he did

Maidstone

There was a young man from Maidstone, Kent
Who once gave up wanking for Lent
When he at last shot his load
His sperm flowed and flowed
For an hour or two till he was spent

Margate

There was a young man from Mar-gate
Who for Lent did not once masturbate
His balls did so ache
And started to quake
Then fell off on account of their weight

Ramsgate

I once asked a friend from Ramsgate
Who spoke German, if he could translate
'*Verpiss Dich*' for me
'Oh piss off!' said he
I said, 'Flipping heck, I only asked, mate'

Rochester

There was a young lady from Rochester
Who I asked if a fuck might interest her
She said, 'Yes it would
We definitely could'
My chat-up line must have impressed her

Royal Tunbridge Wells

From this whorehouse in Royal Tunbridge Wells
Emanated some terrible smells
So bad was the stench
I forwent a wench
And went home with all my sperm cells

Sandwich

There was a young man from Sandwich, Kent
Who once gave up wanking for Lent
Afterwards his sperm shot
From there to Ascot
Before starting its gradual descent

Sevenoaks

There was a young lady from Sevenoaks
Who set a new world record for pokes
She put on a display
And by the end of the day
Had fucked nine hundred and twenty-two blokes

Sheerness

There once was an old man from Sheerness
Tried Viagra without apparent success
But on closer inspection
He found he'd an erection
Every time he saw his sheepdog, Jess

Sittingbourne

A young man from Sittingbourne, Kent
Once gave up wanking for Lent
He felt quite frustrated
And he estimated
His balls had swelled by ten percent

Strood

There once was a young man from Strood
Whose manner was a little bit rude
He'd get his dick out
And wave it about
Whenever he felt in the mood

Tonbridge

There was a young man from Tonbridge, Kent
Who once gave up wanking for Lent
His balls became so loaded
They actually exploded
Much to his eternal lament

Whitstable

There once was a man from Whit-stable
Although it might just be a fable
And his only vice
Was to keep pubic lice
And race them on the dining room table

Lancashire

Accrington

There was a young lady from Accy
Whose habits were really quite whacky
She'd think nothing finer
Than to fill her vagina
With two ounces of chewing tobaccy

Bacup

On my night out in the town of Bacup
I had a bit too much beer to sup
I did perhaps overrate
My choice of bedmate
From the look of with whom I woke up

Barnoldswick

There was a chap from Barnoldswick
With quite a good balancing trick
He'd position two forks
On top of some corks
Then balance the lot on his dick

Blackburn

A young lady from Blackburn in Lancs
Inspired me to have many wanks
I recalled her snatch
That was quite without match
And sent her a note saying thanks

Blackpool

In Blackpool in Lancashire
I saw a magic act on the pier
The conjurer's illusion
Caused himself much confusion
When he made his own balls disappear

Burnley

A young man from Burnley in Lancs
Saved up all the sperm from his wanks
He once showed his mum
He'd stored so much come
That it filled twenty-seven fish tanks

Chorley

Once after a night out in Chorley
I woke up feeling really quite poorly
But worse was to come
When I examined my bum
And found up it a large creepy-crawly

Cleveleys

There was a young man from Cleve-leys
Whose bollocks hung down to his knees
But they'd not get in the way
Because, sad to say
They were the size of two petits pois peas

Clitheroe

Said a young man from Clitheroe
To his girlfriend, an Eskimo
'The frost in December
Plays hell with my member
Do we have to fuck out in the snow?'

Darwen

A question, as a starter for ten:
'Why wasn't Christ born in Dar-wen?'
Well, it seems they were able
To find there a stable
But not a virgin or three wise men

Fleetwood

There was a young man from Fleetwood
Whose balls didn't look like they should
They were so very huge
They produced so much spooge
When he came it was more like a flood

Garstang

A butler who came from Garstang
Once answered his master, 'You rang?'
His master said with a cough
'I've just been wanking off
Now would you please wipe off my wang?'

Lancaster

There was a young man from Lancaster
Who tried to cast his penis in plaster
But he mixed it too thick
It took the skin off his dick
And just ended in painful disaster

Leyland

There once was a whore from Leyland
With one extra mammary gland
If you gave her a fuck
A tit could you suck
Still leaving one for each hand

Lytham St Annes

There was a man from Lytham St Annes
Who was lacking at making of plans
He said, 'I will thank ye
Can I borrow your hanky?
I'm afraid I've just come in my hands'

Morecambe

There was a young man from Morecambe
Who put a hamster up his bum
He said to his pet
'Are you enjoying it yet?
'Cause for me it's not very much fun'

Nelson

This chap from Nelson, Lancashire
Had quite an interesting career
He worked in sperm banking
And his job was just wanking
But it wore him out after a year

Ormskirk

After a day's drinking once in Ormskirk
It was said I behaved like a berk
When I accepted a dare
To walk round the market square
Wearing naught but my socks and a smirk

Oswaldtwistle

I worked in a shop in Oswaldtwistle
But it wasn't long before my dismissal
Which was for slacking off
That and jacking off
In the storeroom, with my throbbing gristle

Penwortham

In Penwortham, which is in South Ribble
One fine day I went out for a nibble
I found a pretty rough whore
Who charged two pound fifty-four
And at that price I wasn't going to quibble

Preston

There was a young lady from Preston
Whose breasts my hand once came to rest on
But she said, 'Get your mitts
From off of my tits
Or I'll throw you from here down to Weston'

Skelmersdale

A young man from Skelmersdale
Caught his knob on a rusty nail
It was quite a shock
To so lose half his cock
And he felt like a second class male

Leicestershire

Ashby-de-la-Zouch

There was a young lady from this place
Whose twat was a most special case
It was so big inside
That at half a mile wide
It broke all laws of physical space

Braunstone Town

There was a young man from Braunstone Town
Who frankly will let this book down
He had no habits sick
A nice normal dick
And two normal balls that were round

Coalville*

There was a young lady from Coal-ville
Who chanced to alight on a mole's hill
The inquisitive mole
Stuck his nose up her hole
The young lady's alright, but the mole's ill

Hinckley

There was a young man from Hinckley
Who thought his penis rather crinkly
Till he gave it redress
With a steam ironing press
Which straightened it out quite distinctly

Leicester

I met a young lady from Leicester
And kissed her and then caressed her
Her body was so nice
But less so the pubic lice
That I later found out did infest her

Loughborough

One time at Loughborough University
There was an orgy with some diversity
Where I got there my oats
But when they brought out the goats
I was less keen on that one perversity

Lutterworth

There was a young lady from Lutterworth
Whose twat had incredible girth
She was walking about
When two twins fell out
And she didn't even notice the birth

Market Harborough

In Market Harborough's town square
I once saw a sight that was rare
A lass with three tits
And what thrilled me to bits
Was the thought of an extra one spare

Melton Mowbray

Melton Mowbray is known for its pies
And I once had one there of some size
A pie quite that big
Used all the bits of the pig
But its cock in there was still a surprise

Oadby

There was a man from Oadby, Leicestershire
Who was stabbed in the balls with a spear
And at A&E
They were quite shocked to see
Another spear stuck up his rear

Shepshed

There was a young man from Shepshed
Who once took a donkey to bed
While giving it one
He was surprised by Mum
And said, 'Mum, have you met my friend Ned?'

Syston

A boastful young man from Syston[†]
Said, 'I must always check my fly's done
Up proper-ly
It's a challenge you see
'Cause my penis is an oversize one'

Wigston Magna

Once in Wigston Magna, Leicestershire
Lived a young man whose knob was quite queer
He would often contend
That it had such a bend
He could fuck himself up his own rear

[†] Which is pronounced 'Sigh-ston', that is with the first syllable
rhyming with 'pie'

Lincolnshire

Barton-upon-Humber

A young lady from Barton-upon-Humber
Had lovers in inordinate number
But she said, 'To be fair
None of them can compare
To the pleasure I get from a cucumber'

Boston

There was a young man from Boston in Lincs
Whose love life was cursed with a jinx
In any time of romance
He'd just come in his pants
And say, 'Instead shall we play tiddlywinks?'

Brigg

There was a young lady from Brigg
With a vagina exceptionally big
A finger or two
Would certainly not do
She'd use her whole arm for a frig

Cleethorpes

There was once an artist from Cleethorpes
Who carved a huge dick out of quartz
And because it impressed
Whenever he dressed
He'd tuck it in his undershorts

Crowle

At toilets in the town of Crowle[†]
With his dick through a glory hole
A chap was left confused
When his member just got used
As a holder for the lavatory roll

Gainsborough

In Gainsborough by the River Trent
Once happened a strange chance event
An elephant stood
On a young man's manhood
Which left it thereafter quite bent

Grantham

In Grantham they held a parade
I dressed up for the masquerade
But my choice of costume
Caused the town's folk to fume
My giant cock suit left them dismayed

[†] Pronounced 'Croal'

Grimsby

One morning in Grimsby docks
I think I caused one or two shocks
I was wandering around
Certain parts of the town
With a hard-on wearing only my socks

Lincoln

There was a young man from Lincoln
Who developed a terrible symptom
From a skin complaint
Which with lack of restraint
Turned his penis a shade of bright crimson

Louth

When I was in Louth, Lincolnshire
I overdid the delay spray, I fear
I lost all feeling in my dick
And did not regain it quick
In fact it took over a year

Market Deeping

There was a man from Market Deeping
Who began with just a spot of peeping
Then sometimes at times
He'd steal bras from clothes lines
Then put them on just for safekeeping

North Hykeham

There was a young man from North Hykeham
Who'd take out his bollocks and strike 'em
When he was asked why
He'd explain with a sigh
'It's just that I really don't like 'em'

Scunthorpe

There once was a pirate from Scunny
With an outlook so unnaturally sunny
When a swipe of a cutlass
Rendered him nutless
His reaction was to find it most funny

Skegness

There was a young man from Skegness
Who trapped his cock in a trouser press
Once it was greased
It was easily released
But it came out in quite some distress

Spalding

There was a young man from Spalding
Who spilt cooking oil that was scalding
In a bit of a botch
It fell in his crotch
And left most of his pubic hair balding

Stamford*

A Stamford man who was called Reg
Was screwing this lass in a hedge
When along came his wife
With a big carving knife
And chopped off his meat and two veg

Wainfleet All Saints*

A young man from Wainfleet All Saints
Once swallowed some samples of paint
All the colours of the spectrum
Burst forth from his rectum
With a colourful lack of restraint

Merseyside

Billinge

There was a young lady from Billinge
Tried to straighten the hair on her minge
But the straighteners had a fault
Which brought things to a halt
And left her with a bit of a singe

Birkenhead

There was a man from Birkenhead
Whose bollocks were made out of lead
As they swung to and back
It's said that they'd clack
And that his dick had a screw thread

Bootle

There was a young man from Bootle
Who gave himself beatings quite brutal
By whacking his cock
With a big lump of rock
Then happily off he would tootle

Crosby

One day in Crosby, Merseyside
This con man took me for a ride
His 'magic love potion'
Was haemorrhoid lotion
And I'd bought a large bottle untried

Formby

In Formby, out in the sand dunes
I spent one or two afternoons
With a lady who'd wank me
But afterwards spank me
Till my bottom looked like a baboon's

Hoylake

There was a young lady from Hoylake
With whom once sweet love I did make
I'd longed to get my mitts
On her lovely big tits
But they fell off because they were fake

Huyton

A young man from Huyton, Merseyside
Surveyed his penis with a great pride
Saying, 'It's of a fine girth
And the length is of worth
But less so those spots up one side'

Kirkby

A man from Kirkby on the River Alt
Had a penis that developed a fault
Instead of spilling semen
It just shook like a demon
And produced the odd bit of rock salt

Knotty Ash

A young man from Knotty Ash
At the swimming pool created a splash
By standing assured
On the high diving board
And merrily taking a slash

Liverpool

A young man from Liverpool
Had a slightly strange use for his tool
For when he was cooking
If no one was looking
He'd use it for stirring the gruel

Maghull

There was a young man from Maghull
Who cared for his dick to the full
He'd clean it twice daily
And each night he'd gaily
Wrap it up in cotton wool

Newton-le-Willows

A young lady from Newton-le-Willows
Said, 'You have to see my dirty pillows'
And then she related
'I've had them armour plated
And they look just like two armadillos'

Southport

There was a young man from Southport
Who took his sporting goods shop to court
Saying that their jock strap
Was so fucking crap
He could sue them for lack of support

St Helens

Two sisters who hailed from St Helens
Were in court and a right pair of felons
But they got off scot free
With a not guilty plea
And by letting the judge see their melons

Wallasey

A young lady from Wallasey
Had breasts that were a sight to see
Her generous mounds
Each weighed thirty-four pounds
And even more odd she had three

Norfolk

Cromer

A well-hung young man from Cromer
Feared getting a full-on boner
As to get one would drain
All the blood from his brain
And he'd risk falling into a coma

Dereham

To his girlfriend said a young man from Dereham
'Will you lick my balls if I smear 'em
With chocolate spread?'
But in reply she said
'You can fuck off I'm not going near 'em'

Diss

At a urinal in the town of Diss
I was happily taking a piss
When a chap said to me
'My, you're hung like a flea'
A remark I felt rather remiss

Fakenham

There was a young man from Fakenham
If you met him there'd be no mistakin' him
His idea of fun
Was baring his bum
Or getting out his bollocks and shakin' em

Great Yarmouth

A chap from Yarmouth by the sea
Was stung on his dick by a bee
Which so swelled his hose
He dressed in Speedos
And walked round as proud as could be

Holt

There once was a young man from Holt
Whose skills you would have to exalt
With much circumspection
And a prior erection
He could use his dick for a pole vault

King's Lynn

There was a young man from King's Lynn
Whose penis was incredibly thin
His favourite treat
Was having winkles to eat
Using his dick for a pin

Norwich

There was a young man from Nor-wich
Who was troubled by a genital itch
Much to his dismay
He scratched his bollocks away
Now he sings in a very high pitch

Swaffham

There was a young lady from Swaffham
Who decided that she screwed too often
So she'd tell her boyfriends
That apart from weekends
From now on she'd only wank off 'em

Thetford

At Thetford town's railway station
I came close to some organ donation
A man with a knife
Said that I'd fucked his wife
And offered me with my castration

North Yorkshire

Filey

There once was a young man from Filey
With bollocks that hung very highly
He'd not sing sopra-no
But if he had a go
He could do a good impression of Kylie

Harrogate

A chap to his wife in Harrogate
Said, 'For tea could you get me some skate'
And whilst you're at the fish shop
I'll be bashing my bishop
I know you hate to see me masturbate'

Knaresborough

In Knaresborough which is in North Yorks
I did pavement art on the sidewalks
But it started to rain
As I coloured the last vein
Of a picture of my penis in chalks

Middlesbrough

In Middlesbrough in the North Riding
A man once gave me a good chiding
He swore on his life
I'd been seen with his wife
Indulging in some sausage-hiding

Pickering

When I was in the town of Pickering
I thought I would buy my dick a ring
But the project was a flop
I couldn't find a sex shop
And all I got in Boots was some snickering

Redcar

There was a young lady from Redcar
Whose tits were the biggest by far
They were so sizeable
She found it advisable
To use scaffolds instead of a bra

Richmond

Once in Richmond on the River Swale
I went to a local artists' sale
Where I had quite a shock
To find models of my cock
Reproduced in 1/40th scale

Ripon

A lady nudist from the town of Ripon
Once did a banana skin slip on
To save her from falling
With pain for him appalling
She used her husband's penis to grip on

Robin Hood's Bay

One dark night in Robin Hood's Bay
A nun to her colleague did say
'I must remember later
To get a proper vibrator
I've near worn this candle away'

Scarborough

From Scarborough on the North Yorkshire coast
I bought an inflatable doll through the post
Despite a puncture repair
The price was quite fair
And fucking her kept me engrossed

Selby

A young man from Selby on the Ouse
Had an ambition to fuck kangaroos
To fulfil his dream
He hit on the scheme
Of attaching some springs to his shoes

Settle

There once was an old man from Settle
Whose bollocks were made out of metal
When frost was about
He'd pop them both out
And warm the pair up in a kettle

Skelton-in-Cleveland

A young man from Skelton-in-Cleve-land
Had an evening that did not go as planned
Before he'd a chance
To get in his girl's pants
He'd unfortunately come in his hands

Skipton

There was a young man from Skipton
Who truly was a well-equipped 'un
He said, 'On my dick I'll get
The entire alphabet
Tattooed in Cyrillic script on'

Stensall*

There was a young man from Stensall
Whose dick was as sharp as a pencil
On the night of his wedding
It went through the bedding
And shattered the chamber utensil

Tadcaster

The 'grow it big' cream I bought from Tadcaster
Was frankly a fucking disaster
It did nothing more
Than to make my dick sore
And require quite a large sticking plaster

Thornaby-on-Tees*

A young lady from Thornaby-on-Tees
Had muff hair that hung down to her knees
The crabs got together
To knit her a sweater
So in winter her twat wouldn't freeze

Whitby

From Whitby on the North Yorkshire coast
I bought an inflatable doll through the post
She had a hole at each end
So I called up a friend
And we both shared her with a spit roast

Yarm

There once was a young man from Yarm
Who worked at the local stud farm
When the stallion was ill
He would for him in fill
And fuck all the mares with his arm

York*

There once was an old man from York
Whose cock was as dry as a cork
When trying to screw
He split it in two
Now he uses the thing as a fork

Northamptonshire

Brackley

I met a young lady from Brackley
And asked her please if she might jack me
Off with her hand
Which I thought would be grand
But in practice she did it quite slackly

Burton Latimer

A young man from Burton Latimer
With his lass was so lacking in stamina
When screwing he would do
Just one stroke or two
Before shooting all his pearl jam in her

Corby

A young lady from Corby, Northants
Had enormously big breast implants
With tits of such size
It was no real surprise
That when I saw them I came in my pants

Daventry

To a dominatrix from Daventry
I said, 'Yes, we can screw if you're free
But this time please promise
Not to whack my John Thomas
With such a big branch from a tree'

Kettering

There was a young man from Kettering
With a tattoo that would take some bettering
He had *The Birth of Venus*
Reproduced on his penis
With the title in copperplate lettering

Northampton

With this dominatrix from Northampton
I felt my ardour slightly dampen
When she said, 'Just relax
I've got here some hot wax
That I'm just going to drip on your Hampton[†]'

[†] Hampton, of course, being a slang term for penis (from the rhyming slang: Hampton = Hampton Wick = dick)

173

Rushden

In Rushden by the River Nene‡
I indulged in behaviour obscene
By playing with my hose
In an aisle of Waitrose
After coating it in their margarine

Thrapston

A young man from Thrapston, Northants
Could piss an amazing distance
He once had a pee
That went too far to see
And landed in the middle of France

Towcester

A well-hung young man from Towcester
Was known to be a bit of a boaster
But if he served you tea
You'd still be surprised to see
A picture of his dick on the coaster

Wellingborough

In Wellingborough on the River Nene
Lived a whore who was terribly keen
After working all night
She said, 'I still feel quite bright
I'll just fuck another nineteen'

---

‡ Which can be pronounced 'Nenn' or 'Neen'. With this limerick and the one for Wellingborough we're relying on the latter pronunciation.

Northumberland

Alnwick

There once was a young man from Alnwick
With a most unusual dick
Though extremely long
Something was quite wrong
As it was only two microns thick

Amble

Once I met a young lady from Amble
And took her on a nice nature ramble
Though we had it away
What ruined my day
Was getting my bollocks caught on a bramble

Ashington

In Ashington there was a miner
Whose wife was a fashion designer
One night to his shock
She dressed him up as a cock
And herself as a six foot vagina

Berwick-upon-Tweed

A couple from Berwick-on-Tweed
Made love at an alarming speed
Their record for full sex
Was six point four secs
Which will take some beating, indeed

Blyth

There was a young man from the Blyth Valley
Whose bollocks did not really tally
The left one was quite small
But the other like a ball
You would find at the bowling alley

Cramlington

There was a baker from Cramling-ton
With a habit that was rather rum
He'd wank off his man sap
Into a bread bap
And say, 'How's that for a sticky bun?'

Morpeth

A wealthy old man from Morpeth
Said with his last dying breath
'It's true my young bride
Has taken me for a ride
But it was fun to be fucked to death'

Prudhoe

There was a farmhand from Prudhoe[†]
Whose fondness for cows made me shudder
He would often relate
How he'd need to masturbate
Ev'ry time he caught a glimpse of an udder

Wooler

There once was a young man from Wooler
Whose love life could not have been duller
He'd never wanked or screwed
Cause he thought both too lewd
And his balls couldn't be any fuller

[†] Which is pronounced 'Prudda' with a short 'u'

Nottinghamshire

Arnold

There was a young man from Ar-nold
Who on an origami course enrolled
At the paper folding art
He was crap from the start
But he could fold up his penis fourfold

Beeston

This young lady from Beeston in Notts
For me did once have the hots
But was put off quite quick
When she noticed my dick
Was covered with one or two spots

Bingham

At this big talent contest in Bingham
Was a lady who'd play songs and sing 'em
While her partner, a man
Held his nuts in his hand
And in time to the music would swing 'em

Cotgrave

There was a young man from Cotgrave
Who was stupid but terribly brave
Quite why he took pains
To wire his dick to the mains
Is something he took to the grave

Eastwood

There was a young man from Eastwood
Whose DIY skills were really not good
He was particularly poor
With a circular saw
And accidentally sliced off his manhood

Hucknall

Hucknall was once known for its pits
And this lass with magnificent tits
If she put them down
In certain parts of the town
They'd need their own parking permits

Kirkby-in-Ashfield

Once in Kirkby in the Ashfield area
I met a young lady from Bulgaria
She was really quite cute
But very hirsute
And I don't think I've seen a minge hairier

Mansfield

There was an old man from Mansfield
Who with a cork kept his arsehole quite sealed
Till one day with a blast
The cork shot from his ass
And landed just near Huddersfield

Newark*

There once was a young man from New-ark
Who went swimming in the sea after dark
Now that unfortunate sire
Sings two octaves higher
As his balls got bit off by a shark

Nottingham

There once was a young man from Nottingham
And you'd not have much trouble in spotting 'im
He had detachable balls
And toured billiard halls
Taking out his bollocks and potting 'em

Retford

A chap from Retford on the River Idle
Up to his young lady did sidle
When much to his shock
She chopped off his cock
Which left him feeling quite suicidal

Stapleford

There was a man from Stapleford, Notts
Who flattened his penis lots and lots
By the time he had finished
Its breadth had so diminished
He could use it to fiddle coin slots

Sutton-in-Ashfield

There was a young lady from Sutton
Whose blouse I was pleased to unbutton
But I was slightly less sure
When she rogered me sore
With a big strap-on dick that she'd put on

Worksop

In mid-shag with a lady from Worksop
Her husband walked in throwing a strop
He cried, 'What are you doing?'
I said, 'Well, we're screwing'
But to be fair to him I offered to stop

Oxfordshire

Abingdon

One summer's day in Abingdon
The vicar and I had a ding-dong
Seems he wasn't the keenest
On 'The Good Ship Venus'
As my choice for the church fete's big sing-song

Banbury

Banbury is famed for its cross
I went there one day at a loss
But found nothing to do
Except go for a poo
Then go home and then have a toss

Bicester

With some friends in the town of Bicester
I was playing a game of naked Twister
When I slipped going for green
I was called obscene
But I really hadn't set out to fist her

Carterton

There was a professor from Carterton
And although you would not find a smarter don
He would go on for hours
About golden showers
A topic you would not want him started on

Chipping Norton

A young lady from Chipping Norton
Wanted a vibrator and bought one
But with the money she had
She said, 'That's too bad
I can only afford but a short 'un'

Didcot

There once was a man from Didcot
Who upset his wife quite a whole lot
He'd been playing away
And when she found out one day
She tied up his dick in a knot

Henley-on-Thames

There was a lass from Henley-on-Thames
Whose tits were a real pair of gems
Never mind double D
Or even double E
Her cup size went up to two Ms

Oxford

In Oxford, that great seat of learning
I slept around, not too discerning
Now thanks to some Miss
Each time I piss
I get a sensation of burning

Thame

I was out drunk one evening in Thame
And returned from the gents, head in shame
Alas I'm not joking
My trousers were soaking
I'd been terribly poor with my aim

Wallingford

In Wallingford Castle Gardens
I asked passers-by for their pardons
For my headache I did take
Some Viagra by mistake
And I kept getting these raging hard-ons

Wantage

The lady wrestler that I met from Wantage
Soon had me at some disadvantage
By week two of our fling
My ass was in a sling
And my penis wrapped up in a bandage

Witney

At the newsagents one day in Witney
In behaviour that didn't befit me
Over a mag made for men
I had a wank there and then
Without asking first if they'd permit me

Rutland

Oakham

I once met this lady from Oakham
Who got out her breasts for me to stroke 'em
Then said, 'Let's have a lay
My husband's away
So you can stand in as a locum'

Uppingham

There was a young lady from Uppingham
Who rather liked pheasants and plucking 'em
Young men from the town
Would bring her birds round
And she'd thank the chaps kindly by fucking 'em

Shropshire

Bridgnorth

There was a young man from Bridgnorth
Who would swing his balls back and forth
Till with a cricket bat
His wife squashed 'em flat
Leaving him buggered thenceforth

Church Stretton

There was a young man from Church Stretton
With a plan that he had his heart set on
To grow his dick by a yard
By stretching it hard
Not something I'd put a large bet on

Clun

One Christmas a young man from Clun
Was careless when cleaning his gun
Whilst gaily singing carols
He set off both barrels
And blew off his balls one by one

Craven Arms

There was a young man from Craven Arms
Who worked in Mediterranean farms
He was paid to pick figs
But instead fucked the pigs
And swore the goats too had their charms

Dawley

There once was a young man from Dawley
Who would always come prematurely
Till he hit on this thing
To tie up with string
His ball sac and knot it securely

Ludlow

There was a young lady from Ludlow in Shrops
Who ate only barley and hops
She found she could piss ale
Which was bottled for sale
And sold in all the local shops

Madeley

In the small town of Madeley in Shrops
I opened one of a string of sex shops
But all was not well
And when dildo sales fell
The venture became one of my flops

Oakengates

In the town of Oakengates in Shrops
I opened one of a string of sex shops
But suffered some falls
In my sales of Ben Wa Balls
And the venture was one of my flops

Shrewsbury

In the town of Shrewsbury in Shrops
I opened one more of my string of sex shops
But suffered some slumps
In my sales of penis pumps
And the venture was one of my flops

Telford

In the large town of Telford in Shrops
I had hopes for the next of my sex shops
But sales weren't fantastic
Of vaginas in plastic
And the venture was one of my flops

Wellington

In the town of Wellington in Shrops
I opened one of a string of sex shops
But lacking sales leads
I sold few anal beads
So the venture was one of my flops

Whitchurch

In the small town of Whitchurch in Shrops
I tried once again with my sex shops
But there were some downswings
In my sales of cock rings
So the venture was the last of such flops

Somerset and Bristol

Bath

There was a professor from Bath
Who employed twenty-five research staff
To measure size and direction
Of his every erection
And to plot the results on a graph

Bridgwater

There was a young man from Bridgwater
Whose balls didn't look like they oughta
He had one giant size plum
But what was really rum
Was it doubled in size every quarter

Bristol

There once was a young man from Bristol
Whose balls were made of Waterford crystal
He'd had them replaced
'Cause once when shit-faced
He'd shot himself in the groin with a pistol

Burnham-on-Sea

There was a chap from Burnham-on-Sea
Who was watching a porn DVD
And got the shock of his life
To find it starred his wife
And the whole of Bristol City FC

Castle Cary

At a talent contest in Castle Cary
There was an act there that I found quite scary
A man sang a song selection
Whilst maintaining an erection
With on the end of it perched a canary

Chard

There once was a young man from Chard
Who found he could only get himself hard
By taking Viagra
On the banks of Niagara
And rubbing his penis with lard

Cheddar

Cheddar is widely famed for its cheese
Which indeed has oft been known to please
But you can't beat a blob
Of the cheese from my knob
You can try some if you're down on your knees

Clevedon

After drinking on a night out in Clevedon
My last idea was a misconceived 'un
What grieved me so sore
Was that I'd paid this whore
But an erection, I couldn't achieve one

Frome

On her wedding night a bride from Frome[†]
Said, 'I don't think that much of my groom
I was more satisfied
When sitting astride
The handle I found on a broom'

Glastonbury

At Glastonbury Festival last year
I acted upon quite a bum steer
Fearing I'd been caught
With drugs of some sort
I shoved four Oxo cubes up my rear

Keynsham

At the B&B I stayed in at Keyn-sham
At breakfast the landlady said, 'Damn!
I'm not much of a host
There's nothing for the toast'
So I offered to produce her pearl jam

[†] Pronounced 'Froom'

Minehead*

There was a sailor from Minehead
Who once took a mermaid to bed
He said, 'To be blunt
I can't find your cunt
So why don't you blow me instead'

Nailsea

The lady wrestler I met from Nailsea
Was a little bit too much for me
We had this one tussle
Where she pulled my love muscle
Till I wailed like a screaming banshee

Norton Radstock

At a rainbow's end in Newton Radstock
I went searching for gold in a crock
But fate was unkind
And all that I did find
Was a leprechaun wanking his cock

Portishead

There was a young man from Portishead
Who put terrible things on his bread
Of his smegma mixed with cream
He said, 'It works like a dream
And makes a nice tasty cheese spread'

Taunton*

A lady from Taunton in Somerset
Once inspected me through her lorgnette
She said, 'Your dick's unsurpassed
I must take a cast
It'll make such a fine statuette'

Wellington

At a boot throwing contest held in Wellington
I was hit by a straying Wellington
I shouted out, 'Crumbs!
That's caught me in the plums
Causing me a pain and swelling one'

Wells

The fondness of this chap from Wells
For animals should have rung alarm bells
Before he ran off to elope
With Bristol Zoo's antelope
Their gorilla and a herd of gazelles

Weston-super-Mare

There was a young lady from Weston
Whose breasts my hand came to rest on
But she said, 'Get your mitts
From off of my tits
Or I'll throw you from here up to Preston'

Yeovil

There was a young man from Yeo-vil
Who was blessed with an unusual skill
Whilst some in fits and starts
Can do musical farts
He could fart whole concertos at will

South Yorkshire

Askern

There was a young man from Askern
Who said to his lass, 'I'll never learn
If I screw you once more
On this here piece of floor
This'll be the world's worst carpet burn'

Barnsley

There was man from Barnsley, South Yorks
Who tried to have sex with his hawks
But his pecker got pecked
And his bollocks quite wrecked
Which accounts for the way he now walks

Doncaster

There was a young lady from Doncaster
Said to her man, 'Can't you fuck me faster?
If that stew's overcooked
The dinner will be fucked
And this evening will be a disaster'

Hoyland

There was once a whore from Hoyland
Whose services were much in demand
But when her price for a screw
Was just two pound fifty-two
The demand you could quite understand

Maltby*

In Maltby the wife of a miner
Once mistook her mouth for her vagina
Her clitoris huge
She covered with rouge
And lipsticked her labia minor

Mexborough

DIY shopping in Mexborough, South Yorks
The assistant had the most lovely norks
I asked her for a screw
But she said, 'Try aisle two,
Fixings and plasterers' hawks'

Rotherham

DIY shopping in Rotherham, South Yorks
I was admiring the assistant's nice norks
I said, this time very clear
'Would you like a screw, dear?'
But she attacked me with two gardening forks

Sheffield

With this whore from Sheffield, the steel city
I said to her, 'That's rather a pity
I've paid you for fun
But I've already come
After just a quick glimpse of one titty'

Thorne

There once was a young man from Thorne
Who permanently had the horn
So they'd use his stiff 'third leg'
As an impromptu peg
For games of hoopla on the lawn

Wombwell

A boastful young man from Wombwell†
Said, 'Not only can my dick come well
It's reasonably long
And sufficiently strong
I could use it to lift up a dumbbell'

---

† Pronounced locally 'Wum-well'

Staffordshire

Biddulph

A young man from Biddulph in Staffs
Desired to have sex with giraffes
But it just drove him madder
To keep falling off his ladder
In a string of embarrassing gaffes

Burntwood

There was a young man from Burntwood
Whose balls didn't look like they should
One was so big and round
It weighed half a pound
And made his other one look like a dud

Burton upon Trent*

There was a man from Burton-on-Trent
Whose wife fucked the landlord for rent
But as she got older
The landlord grew colder
And so now they live out in a tent

Cannock

There was a young man from Cannock Chase
Who did everything arse about face
His attempts at kerb-crawling
Were frankly appalling
As he drove at a very fast pace

Hednesford

A young man from Hednesford in Staffs
Was so keen on practical maths
If he had an erection
He'd give it close inspection
And plot the findings on some graphs

Kidsgrove

There was a young lady from Kidsgrove
To whom I was nearly betrothed
But I ended my wooing
When I caught her screwing
These three chaps in kilts from Montrose

Leek

There was a young man from Leek
With a strange masturbation technique
He'd soak his dick for a day
In the best delay spray
And have a wank that would take him a week

Lichfield

There was a man from Lichfield Cathedral
Whose bollocks were shaped tetrahedral
To make 'em more round
He'd bash 'em and pound
But at best they became octahedral

Newcastle-under-Lyme

A young man from Newcastle-under-Lyme
If you believe what is said in this rhyme
Was born with two dicks
And he had two chicks
Who he could fuck both at the same time

Rugeley

There once was a young man from Rugeley
Whose dick size would vary quite hugely
On a wet afternoon
It could shrivel like a prune
But the next day be the biggest in Rugeley

Stafford

In Stafford nearby the M6
I once met this dominatrix
Who fuck her she'd let me
But slightly upset me
By bashing my balls with two bricks

Stoke-on-Trent

There once was a young man from Stoke
Who when wanking was going for broke
It might be a fiction
But it was said the friction
Caused his manhood to go up in smoke

Stone

There was a young lady from Stone
Whose breasts each weighed nearly a stone
I've oft heard it said
They'd used implants of lead
'Cause they'd run out of sili-cone

Tamworth

There was a young man from Tam-worth
Who'd a notion he thought might cause mirth
He painted his cock in blue
With the bell end a white hue
And tried to pass it off as a Smurf

Uttoxeter

There was a fair young maid from Uttoxeter
Men would shower jewellery and frocks at her
But she cared not for such things
And wanted sex without strings
So now they all just wave their cocks at her

Suffolk

Beccles

There was a young lady from Beccles
Whose twat was all covered in freckles
With all those spots
You could play join the dots
And she'd let you if you had the shekels

Bungay

There one was a young man from Bungay[†]
Who tied a rope to his dick to jump bungee
In the hope to lengthen it
Which it didn't do a bit
But it did make it rather more spongy

Bury St Edmunds

There was a young man from Bury
Who was desperate to lose his cherry
I saw he looked glum
So offered my bum
But the offer did not please him very

---

† Which is pronounced 'Bungy' with a hard 'g'

Felixstowe

There was a man from Felixstowe
Who attended his first live bed show
And got the shock of life
To see there his wife
On stage fucking her tennis pro

Haverhill

There was a whore from Haverhill
Who left me her twat in her will
To preserve her slit
In the fridge I put it
I think it's at the back of it still

Ipswich

There was a young lady from Ipswich
Had the most adorable lips, which
She wrapped round my cock
Then said to my shock
'You can come on my bum or my nips, which?'

Lowestoft

There was an old chap from Lowestoft
Who thought his dick now permanently soft
When one day with surprise
A hard-on met his eyes
And he paraded with it proudly aloft

Mildenhall

There was a young man from Mildenhall
Who was trespassing over a wall
Topped with broken glass
On which he caught his arse
And sliced off his cock and a ball

Newmarket

At Newmarket one day at the races
I said to this chap, 'Could we change places?
Your wife looks so fine
And I don't fancy mine
Now her arse takes up two seating places'

Stowmarket

In Stowmarket on the River Gipping
My lady friend my penis was gripping
But her wanking technique
Made me damn near shriek
Till we greased her hand with beef dripping

Sudbury

There was a young man from Sud-bury
Who'd eat nothing but vindaloo curry
The truth to tell
This made him unwell
And for weeks he'd shit nothing but slurry

Surrey

Addlestone

A biologist from Addlestone
His own penis he managed to clone
Now he has two dicks
With which he can perform tricks
And is becoming pretty well known

Ashford*

In Ashford there was this commuter
Who could often be seen on his scooter
His favourite trick
Was to stand on his prick
And use his arse as a hooter

Camberley

A lady at the Camberley Obelisk
Said to her chap, 'We'll keep this shag brisk
We're in public so
This time we'll forego
The rubber gloves and the egg whisk'

Caterham

In Caterham in the North Downs
Lived this lass with luverly mounds
She would show you her nips
For one bag of chips
And the rest for just two or three pounds

Dorking

When I stayed in the town of Dorking
My neighbour and I got to talking
I kept coming back
'Cause she had a nice rack
And before very long we were porking

Epsom

An autoeroticist from Epsom
Got a banana stuck up his bum
After procedures protracted
It was at last extracted
Along with two pears and a plum

Ewell

There once was a young man from Ewell
Who got thrown out of veterinary school
He'd done well in classes
But was over-fond of asses
And had been caught fucking this mule

Farnham*

A young man from near Farnham castle
Once wrapped up a shit in a parcel
He sent it by train
With a note to explain
That it came from his grandmother's arsehole

Godalming

There was a young man from Godalming
Who could do an incredible thing
He could twist his dick
Right round a stick
Until it looked just like a spring

Guildford

At McDonald's in Guildford in Surrey
I spilt coffee on my crotch in a scurry
I had to act quick
To cool down my dick
So I stuck it into my McFlurry

Horley

I met a young lady from Horley
Who was up for fucking most surely
But my passion ignited
I got over excited
And came in my pants prematurely

Redhill

There once was a chap from Redhill
Who possessed an unusual skill
He'd balance a pint of draught
On his erect penis shaft
And never a drop would he spill

Reigate*

There was a young man from Reigate
Whose dick it was so true and straight
That the navy when fighting
Could use it for sighting
And at full range could sink a frigate

Staines*

There was a young man from Staines
More blessed with bollocks than brains
He stood on a stool
To bugger a mule
And got kicked in the balls for his pains

Weybridge

There was a young man from Weybridge
Who was bit on his dick by a midge
He was heard to utter
'If I rub it with butter
It might ease the itching a smidge'

Woking

My talk was meant to be thought-provoking
When I addressed this meeting in Woking
But alas not. Unwise,
I had not checked my flies
And my penis was out of them poking

Tyne and Wear

Gateshead

An unfortunate chap from Gateshead
Found his pubic lice rather widespread
They had multiplied
And now occupied
The hair on his chest and his head

Hebburn

There once was a whore from Heb-burn
Whose business was a thriving concern
They'd queue up round the blocks
For her to please their cocks
And I had to queue three days for my turn

Hetton-le-Hole

Alas my lady friend from Hetton-le-Hole
Told me she'd no longer use for my pole
Saying she'd rather straddle
Her Sybian saddle
Which didn't leave a mess in her hole

Houghton-le-Spring

With a lady from Houghton-le-Spring
I was screwing away in full swing
When in walked her husband Bob
Who said, 'You've saved me a job
When you've finished would you like a gin sling?'

Jarrow

There was a young lady from Jarrow
Whose twat was a little too narrow
She got through the love lube
By tube after tube
So she had it delivered by barrow

Longbenton

There was a young man from Longbenton
Who oddly enough had a long bent 'un
Which was from a mishap
When the unfortunate chap
Had his dick most badly leant on

Newcastle upon Tyne

I tried busking one day in Newcastle
With a strategy really quite facile
I sang simple songs
Whilst swinging my dong
With the end of it sporting a tassel

North Shields

A young man from North Shields on Tyne
Had an odd way of passing the time
He'd give his knob a good clean
With a spot of Mr Sheen
And polish the bell end to a shine

Ryton

There once was a young man from Ryton
Who was not an incredibly bright 'un
To his girlfriend's shrugs
He'd labelled her jugs
'L' and 'R' to tell the left from the right 'un

South Shields

A young man from South Shields on the Tyne
Had an odd way of passing the time
He'd paint his dick blue
Or some other hue
Then clean it off with turpentine

Sunderland

'You might find this hard to understand'
Said a masochist from Sunderland
'But whacking my dick
With my wife's hockey stick
Is my idea of absolute wonderland'

Tynemouth

One day I was at Tynemouth Longsands
With plenty of time on my hands
There was little to do
Except have a wank or two
Whilst thinking of mammary glands

Wallsend

If you go to the town of Wallsend
There's a whore there I can recommend
An excellent fuck
And if you're in luck
She might bring along her best friend

Washington

When in Washington, Tyne and Wear
I had a great time, but I fear
The itching I get
Means the lady I met
Left me crabs for a nice souvenir

Whitley Bay*

A virgin from Whitley Bay
Emerged from her bath in dismay
For she'd been deflowered
When she bent as she showered
'Cause the handle was right in her way

Warwickshire

Atherstone

To my girl at the Atherstone hunt
I said, 'I don't know what it's like for your cunt
But they're squeezing my cobblers
These overtight jodhpurs
I may have them on back to front'

Bedworth

There was a young man from Bedworth
And of bollocks he had quite a dearth
Both of his knackers
Were blown off with firecrackers
An event that did not cause him mirth

Henley-in-Arden

A young man from Henley-in-Arden
Got excited at botanical gardens
If he had such turns
He'd sneak behind ferns
To hide away his raging hard-ons

Kenilworth

I met a lady by Kenilworth clock
Who went on to play with my cock
Which I really enjoyed
But she was quite annoyed
When I came on her best summer frock

Leamington Spa

A young man from Leamington Spa
Had balls that were very bizarre
He could take them out his sac
And then put them back
And he kept them at home in a jar

Nuneaton

There was a young man from Nuneaton
Who really enjoyed being beaten
And squeezing his knackers
With a pair of nut crackers
And riding a bike with no seat on

Rugby

In Rugby the home of the game
I stood up to proudly proclaim
A fart-lighting contest
With a prize for the best
And bonus for a nice coloured flame

Stratford-upon-Avon

At a fete held in Stratford-upon-Avon
The organisers at me were raving
It seems they didn't approve
And said I must remove
My stall offering pubic hair shaving

Warwick

I met a young lady from Warwick
And we enjoyed a very nice frolic
But we found to our grief
That we had used a sheath
With a use-by-date somewhat historic

Whitnash

At a bookshop one day in Whitnash
I found an amazing porn stash
I bought the whole lot
And raced home at a trot
To give the old bishop a bash

West Midlands

Birmingham*

There once was a bishop from Birmingham
Who rogered three maids whilst confirming 'em
As they knelt on the hassock
He lifted his cassock
And slipped his episcopal worm in 'em

Bloxwich

The delay spray I bought in Bloxwich
Was according to the salesman's sales pitch
Said to becalm my donger
So I could screw longer
But all it did was make my knob itch

Brierley Hill

With this young lady from Brierley Hill
The evening went well up until
She went flipping bonkers
And kneed me in the conkers
When I couldn't pay the restaurant bill

Brownhills

One night in the town of Brownhills
I took some rather strange pills
It is my recollection
I had a week long erection
And my nuts went all hard like Brazils

Coventry

There was a young man from Coven-try
Whose dick hung down below his knee
When erect, he'd a pole
Too big for any hole
But it could keep up a fair-sized marquee

Darlaston

There was a young man from Dar-last-on
Whom fortune had unkindly passed on
Whilst wanking on a stool
He slipped and broke his tool
Which explains why his dick has a cast on

Dudley

I once bathed with a lady from Dudley
But just as we were getting cuddly
The moment went wrong
When I emitted a pong
Making the water go bubbly

Halesowen

There was a young man from Halesowen
Who would masturbate without slowing
His beating his meat
Would produce so much heat
The end of his knob would be glowing

Sedgley

A young lady from Sedgley Beacon
With whom the pleasure I was seeking
Stopped me to say
'What about the foreplay?
At least first give my nipples a tweaking'

Smethwick

There was a young man from Smethwick
With a rather unusual dick
It was so long and thin
It came up to his chin
And he'd use the thing as a toothpick

Solihull

There was a young man from Solihull
Who thought that his bell end looked dull
With an idea unwise
That bought tears to his eyes
He polished it up with wire wool

Stourbridge

In Stourbridge that is known for its glass
Lived a lady whose manners were crass
She once met the Queen
And said, 'How are you old bean?'
Before emitting a noise from her ass

Sutton Coldfield

To a cross-dressing friend from Sutton
I said, 'You look like lamb done up mutton
I don't mean to be unkind
Your make-up is fine
It's just those plastic breasts that you've put on'

Tipton

At a naturist club in Tipton
As my vodka and lime I sipped on
The sight caught my eye
Of a man passing by
With a dick so long it got tripped on

Walsall*

There was a young man from Walsall
Whose prick was exceedingly small
When in bed with a lay
He could screw her all day
Without touching the vaginal wall

Wednesbury

I made an error one night in Wednesbury
After chopping chillies for the curry
To give hand washing a miss
Before taking a piss
And my dick was on fire in a hurry

Wednesfield

There was a young man from Wednesfield
To whom 'water sports' once appealed
But his first golden shower
Left him feeling quite dour
And considered his decision repealed

West Bromwich

A young lady from West Bromwich
Had a ride-on sex toy with a glitch
It alas gave her minge
An unfortunate singe
Each time she turned on its switch

Willenhall

I met these three whores from Willenhall
And I certainly found it a thrill and all
When all of them said
I could take them to bed
And for the price of one I could drill 'em all

Wolverhampton

A young man from Wolverhampton
Said, 'Something's obstructing my Hampton'
'Oh' said his lass
'You'd better do my ass
My cunt's occupied with a tampon'

West Sussex

Bognor Regis

On a day out in Bognor Regis
For a swim I just took off my breeches
But as I'd gone commando
All was on show
And I got myself thrown off their beaches

Burgess Hill

A young lady from Burgess Hill
Had a desire she tried to fulfil
First with a small vibrator
Then ten minutes later
Her two foot long ground pepper mill

Chichester

A young man who hailed from Chichester
Thought himself quite the local jester
When he said, 'If you please
How's this for knob cheese'
And carved a cock out of Red Leicester

Crawley

A young lady from the town of Crawley
Said to her young man most demurely
'Alas I won't dance tonight
This bra's not quite right
As it holds my tits most insecurely'

East Grinstead

A nymphomaniac from East Grinstead
Would fill local men up with dread
Because legend would tell
That although they'd been well
She'd fucked at least twenty chaps dead

Haywards Heath

A young lady from Haywards Heath
Was most expert at hand relief
With just a couple of strokes
She'd finish most blokes
At a speed that was beyond belief

Horsham

In Horsham on the River Arun
My love life was a little barren
Till I met this girl Sue
Who said, 'I'll gladly screw you
If I can bring along my mate Karen'

Littlehampton

There was a young man from Littlehampton
Who one day got his wanger stamped on
Off most of it snapped
So he had to adapt
To having quite a little Hampton

Shoreham-by-Sea

There was a young lady from Shoreham
With tits so big you couldn't ignore 'em
A team of mountaineers
Got lost there for years
After they had set out to explore 'em

Southwick

At a social function once in Southwick
They gave me a good deal of stick
When I returned from the gents
Without having the sense
To check I'd put away my dick

Worthing

I once stopped at a diner in Worthing
But did not like the look of my serving
The sausage gave me a shock
It looked just like my cock
Which I found a little unnerving

West Yorkshire

Baildon

I knew a young lady from Baildon
Who could nearly always be prevailed on
Whenever in the town
I'd be sure to pop round
And my member she'd soon be impaled on

Batley

There was a young lady from Batley
Who looked a lot like Clement Attlee
With moustache and bald head
No one took her to bed
The boys would all turn her down flatly

Bingley

There once was a whore from Bingley
Who'd take chaps in pairs or them singly
Or sometimes three or four
For which she'd charge more
And save it in the Bradford and Bingley[†]

[†] Clearly this must have been before the former building society, the Bradford and Bingley, was nationalised and its savings business sold on.

Bradford*

A Bradford man who was called Reg
Was fucking this lass in a hedge
When along came his wife
With a big carving knife
And chopped off his meat and two veg

Brighouse

A young lady who hailed from Brighouse
Said to her chap, 'I'm not one to grouse
But you came a bit quick
And I don't like your dick
I've seen bigger ones on a mouse'

Castleford*

In Castleford the wife of a miner
Had an enormous vagina
And when she was dead
They painted it red
And used it for docking a liner

Cleckheaton

There was young lady from Cleckheaton
Who complained to her friend, a discrete 'un
'The dildoes you lend me
Are too fucking bendy
I'd like a reinforced concrete 'un'

Dewsbury

In the town of Dewsbury, West Yorks
I gave one of my specialist talks
Giving a presentation
On techniques of masturbation
Over pictures of girls with big norks

Featherstone

There was a young man from Featherstone
Who once tried to fuck his trombone
But on moving the slide
His cock was sucked inside
And he let forth a discordant tone

Halifax

At a beauticians once in Halifax
They had a special on back, sac and cracks
They did them half price
If they thought your dick nice
And you didn't mind them using old wax

Heckmondwike

An exhibitionist from Heckmondwike
Would often go nude on a hike
Till he caught on one ramble
His nuts on a bramble
Which was something he did not much like

Holmfirth

I found little to do in Holmfirth
And nothing there to cause me mirth
So to relieve the boredom
I played with my organ
And wanked it for all it was worth

Huddersfield

In Huddersfield in the West Riding
It didn't take too much deciding
When this lass said to me
'Would you prefer more tea
Or that I give your cock a good riding'

Ilkley*

A young lady from Ilkley Moor
Found that she just couldn't score
To please her socket
She mounted a rocket
And came with a colossal roar

Keighley

To his butler, the Twelfth Earl of Keighley‡
Said, 'I've just had the maid underneath me
But it's a bit of a bugger
To get off this rubber
Could you please assist and unsheath me?'

---

‡ Pronounced 'Keeth-lee'. Also there isn't actually an Earl of Keighley
– that's artistic license!

Leeds*

There was a young lady from Leeds
Who swallowed a packet of seeds
Within an hour
Her twat was in flower
But her arse was all covered in weeds

Mirfield

In Mirfield on the River Calder
A chap got his dick trapped by a boulder
When he'd stretched the thing free
It hung below his knee
So he kept it tossed over his shoulder

Morley

I went to the doctors in Morley
It was not that I was feeling poorly
As I explained with cough
I just couldn't get off
The Arab strap I'd put on securely

Otley

There was once a whore from Otley
Whose clientele were rather motley
From a man with two dicks
To a dominatrix
But she pleased them all reasonably hotly

Pontefract

There was a chap from Pontefract
Who caught me and his wife in the act
It ended in farce
With his boot up my arse
Which it took me a while to extract

Shipley

At a garden party once in Shipley
I proposed, 'Why don't we all just strip free
Of our clothes and be nude
And do things that are lewd?'
But they told me they'd much rather sip tea

Todmorden

There once was a whore from Todmorden
Around whom they put up a cordon
She had genital warts
And STDs of all sorts
All of which she'd caught from the Churchwarden

Wakefield

Near Wakefield in the West Riding
I did a spot of naked hang-gliding
But felt much less keener
After I'd caught my wiener
On a pylon I hadn't seen hiding

Wetherby

There was a young lady from Wetherby
The most flexible one there might ever be
It was her favourite stunt
To put her head up her cunt
Which was something I thought that I'd never see

Wiltshire

Calne

In Calne in the North Wessex Downs
At Tesco's I caused one or two frowns
By getting an erection
In the bakery section
Whilst thinking of my lady friend's mounds

Chippenham

There was a young man from Chippenham
Whose flies he would never be zippin' 'em
Which was rather un-neat
But he was scared to repeat
The time that he once caught his dick in 'em

Corsham*

There once was a man from Corsham
Who took out his bollocks to wash 'em
His wife said, 'Jack,
If you don't put 'em back
I'll stand on the bastards and squash 'em'

Devizes[*]

There was a young man from Devizes
Whose bollocks were different sizes
One was so small
It was no ball at all
But the other was big and won prizes

Melksham

There was a young man from Melk-sham
Who would always act the big 'I am'
The reason for his pride
Was his balls of such size
That he carried them round in a pram

Salisbury[*]

There once was a curate of Sarum[†]
Whose conduct was quite harum-scarum
He ran about Hants
Without any pants
Till compelled by his bishop to wear 'em

Swindon

There was a young lady from Swindon
Who I once accidentally broke wind on
I said, 'Pardon my guts'
But she kneed me in the nuts
Which was not what I had my hopes pinned on

[†] To use here the ancient name for the city

Trowbridge

A young man from Trowbridge in Wilts
Explained thus his fondness for kilts:
'My bits can swing free
As short people can see
When I go around walking on stilts'

Warminster

There was a young man from Warminster
Who was locally known as just 'Stinker'
For his regular bouts
Of just eating sprouts
And the lack of control of his sphincter

Wootton Bassett

A librarian from Wootton Bassett
Suffered badly with wind and would pass it
But before every fart
He'd hold his arse cheeks apart
In the hope it would keep his farts tacit

Worcestershire

Bromsgrove

A tapestry maker from Bromsgrove
Was quite an eccentric old cove
He would always depict
The image of his dick
In each bit of weaving he wove

Droitwich Spa

A sex worker from Droitwich Spa
Advised me I could take off her bra
And enjoy a tit wank
For just one Swiss Franc
Four pounds and a Serbian Dinar

Evesham

A young man from Evesham, Worcestershire
Kept his foreskin as a souvenir
From the day he caught his cock
On a rather sharp rock
And turned roundhead from cavalier

Kidderminster

A young man from Kidderminster
Would really feel the cold every winter
Usually his pains
Were just simple chilblains
But one year got frostbite on his winkler

Malvern

At a garden centre once in Mal-vern
I received a rebuke that was stern
I had been caught short
But guess I shouldn't have ought
To have pissed behind one of their ferns

Pershore

There was a young man from Pershore
Who caught his knob in a revolving door
A problem indeed
But when finally freed
Its length had been stretched by times four

Redditch

A young man from Redditch, Worcestershire
Had a party trick after some beer
To swing by his dick
Most acrobatic
From the town hall's antique chandelier

Stourport-on-Severn

At a garden party once in Stourport
They talked of ailments of all sorts
But I dropped a social clanger
When I got out my wanger
To show them my genital warts

Worcester

There was a young man from Worcester
Who only an erection could muster
If he first got his chick
To tickle his dick
With a forty-eight inch feather duster

Wythall

There was a young man from Wythall
Who lost his sexual parts in a fall
To this lady, a looker
He said he'd like to fuck her
But no longer had the wherewithal

Wales

Clwyd

Abergele

There was a young man from Abergele
Who was stung by bees all up his belly
He also got stung
Where his private parts hung
Now when he comes he produces royal jelly

Buckley

A mercenary from Buckley, Flintshire
Became a bit less cavalier
When his organ most prized
Got roughly circumcised
By an opponent wielding a spear

Colwyn Bay

At a party held in Colwyn Bay
There were games to excite the soiree
But I came in last place
With an arse in my face
When naked Twister we did play

Conwy

There was a young man from Conwy†
Who wanked to a shocking degree
From the moment he'd woken
His cock he'd be strokin'
From dawn till at least half past three

Deeside

There was a young man from Deeside
Whose penis had holes up one side
His girlfriend, to boot
Would play it as a flute
If the sheet music you could provide

Flint

An inexperienced young man from Flint
Surveying his private parts with a squint
Said, 'I wish I could be sure
I knew what these things were for
I wish someone would give me a hint'

Llandudno

On a day out at Llandudno Bay
I walked round with my dick on display
Till a feeling of cold
Began to take hold
And I reluctantly put it away

---

† Which can be pronounced 'Conway' or 'Conwee'. For this limerick we're relying on the latter pronunciation.

Mold

A wife to her husband from Mold
Said, 'How our love life has grown cold
The passion's expired
Now that we have retired
And your dick is all covered in mould'

Prestatyn

A young lady from the town of Prestatyn
Her vagina she kept her pet rat in
But when one day her pet
Would not out of it get
She decided she must send the cat in

Rhyl

Said a husband to his wife from Rhyl
'Is our love life no longer a thrill?
The next time we fuck
At least put down your book
And don't keep on reading it still'

Wrexham

A dominatrix up in Wrexham
Whips her clients and then subjects 'em
To tortures untold
Which would leave me cold
But her customers' dicks it erects 'em

Dyfed

Aberystwyth*

A young lady from Aberystwyth
Took grain to the mill to get grist with
The miller's son Jack
Laid her flat on her back
And united the organs they pissed with

Cardigan

There was an old man from Cardigan
Who said, 'I'll never get my dick hard again
If Viagra doesn't work
I'll just go berserk
And try rubbing it over with lard again'

Carmarthen

A sculptor from the town of Carmarthen
Worked in wood to keep him from starvin'
But statuettes of his dick
Didn't sell out very quick
Despite the fineness of the carving

Fishguard*

A sailor from Fishguard in Wales
Was an expert at pissing in gales
He could piss in a jar
From the top gallant spar
Without even wetting the sails

Goodwick

There was a young man from Goodwick
Not blessed with a very good dick
It would only get hard
If he rubbed it with lard
After strapping it up to a stick

Haverfordwest

A young lady from Haverfordwest
With a musical vagina was blessed
She would lift up her gown
And do 'Knees up Mother Brown'
Then ask out for any requests

Laugharne*

A young lady from the town of Laugharne†
Said, 'Oh, how my twat's lost its charm
A finger or two
Used to quite do
Now it takes half of my arm'

---

† Pronounced 'Larn'

Llanelli

A young lady from Llanelli[‡]
Wanked me off rather too deftly
I came very quick
And afterwards my dick
Had friction burns on it she'd left me

Milford Haven

A masochist from Milford Haven
Without any doubt was a most brave 'un
With his balls on the table
He'd have his wife Mabel
Whack them with a big slab of paving

Pembroke[*]

The dick of this chap from Pembroke[††] it
Was quite so long he could suck it
He said with a grin
As he wiped off his chin
If my ear was a cunt I could fuck it

St Clears

There was a duchess from St Clears
Who for lovers had few volunteers
Because once she was sated
She'd have them castrated
To keep their balls as souvenirs

[‡] Pronounced approximately 'Lan-ethly', although neither the 'L' nor the 'th' in that approximation really do justice to the Welsh 'll' sound.
[††] Pronounced 'Pem-brook'

Tenby

To his girlfriend a young man from Tenby
Said 'Your politics doesn't offend me
But what might our love ruin
Is the fact that you're screwing
At least half of the Welsh Assembly'

Gwent

Abergavenny*

There was a whore from Abergavenny
Whose usual charge was a penny
For a half of that sum
You could roger her bum
An economy practised by many

Abertillery

A young lady from Abertillery
Worked milking cows at the dairy
Which had left her equipped
With a very strong grip
So a hand job from her could be scary

Bargoed

There was a young man from Bargoed†
Who tried to have sex with a cod
But enacting his wish
Got the wrong end of the fish
And found it bit off his love rod

---

† Which can apparently be pronounced in a number of different ways.
For this limerick we're relying on the Welsh pronunciation 'Bar-god'.

Blackwood

There was a young lady from Blackwood
And if you wouldn't I definitely would
One look at her legs
And her chapel hat pegs
And my manhood immediately stood

Caerphilly

A miserly chap from Caerphilly
Said, 'Paying for cheese would be silly
I find plenty enough
For free, of the stuff
When I scrape the smegma off of my willy'

Caldicot*

A maiden aunt from Caldicot
Was alarmed when her nipples grew hot
She had let her tits droop
In her clam chowder soup
So she tied them both up in a knot

Chepstow

A lady vampire from Chepstow
Would oft drink her own menstrual flow
She said it was nice
Served with vodka and ice
And a dash perhaps of Tabasco

Cwmbran

A strange penis enlargement plan
Was devised by this chap from Cwmbran
Who not being too bright
Jumped from a great height
With a rope tied up to his old man

Ebbw Vale

A young man from Ebbw Vale
Put his dick up on eBay for sale
But when bidding was done
He found it no fun
To chop off to post in the mail

Monmouth

There was a young lady from Monmouth
Whose manners were a little bit rough
If not picking her nose
And wiping it on her clothes
She'd be doing likewise with her muff

Newport

A vicar from Newport in Gwent
Got erections wherever he went
Just last Sunday in church
He felt his dick lurch
And could not hide his big trouser tent

Pontypool

There was a young man from Pontypool
Who was thrown out of technical school
For playing fast and loose
And equipment misuse
When he once used his dick as a rule

Risca

There was a young lady from Risca
With hand jobs that couldn't be brisker
If she'd gone any faster
I'd have needed a plaster
I kept the skin on my dick by a whisker

Tredegar

By the time I arrived at Tredegar
I was broke but still sexually eager
Despite being so randy
I settled for a hand shandy
On account that my funds were so meagre

Ystrad Mynach

A young lady from Ystrad Mynach
Any sense of decorum did lack
At high social functions
With little compunction
She would usually get out her rack

Gwynedd

Bangor

There was a young man from Bangor
Who had the most enormous wanger
But it was nothing at all
Compared to his balls
Which would fill up an aeroplane hangar

Blaenau Ffestiniog

There was a man from Blaenau Ffestiniog
Who tried to make love to his dog
But was caused quite some grief
By the sharpness of its teeth
When he tried to give his pit bull a snog

Caernarfon

Caernarfon is known for its castle
And was where I behaved like an asshole
Walking round all day
With my dick on display
On the end of it twirling a tassel

Holyhead

A dominatrix from Holyhead
Was happy to take me to bed
But when I felt her whip
On the end of my dick
I suggested we played cards instead

Llanfairpwllgwyngyllgogerychwyrndrob -wllllantysiliogogogoch

With this limerick for Llanfairpwllgwyngyllgogerychwyrn-
drobwllllantysiliogogogoch
I hit a big stumbling block
For even by the time
I'd written just the first line
The scanning had all gone to cock

Porthmadog

One Christmas time spent in Porthmadog
For five days I didn't go to the bog
When eventual-ly
I let my bowels free
I produced an enormous yule log

Pwllheli

In Pwllheli at the holiday camp
I met this lass who was a vamp
I thrilled to her touch
And we did it so much
That even my penis got cramp

Mid Glamorgan

Aberdare

A young lady from Aberdare
Had the world's bushiest pubic hair
Without a trim
It'd grow from her quim
Till it stood out three foot in the air

Bridgend

When I was in the town of Bridgend
I chose quite the wrong chap to befriend
As we shot the breeze
He spoke of his knob cheese
And showed me it on his bell end

Maesteg

There was a young man from Maesteg
Who taught his dog to sit up and beg
And took to explaining
As reward-based training
He would then let the dog hump his leg

Merthyr Tydfil*

In Merthyr there once was a miner
Who wasn't a very good climber
He slipped on a rock
Fell on his cock
And now he has a vagina

Mountain Ash

My lady friend from Mountain Ash
Was not a fan of my new moustache:
'It don't make you look burly
And the hairs are so curly
Your mouth looks a bit like my gash'

Pencoed

The young lady I met from Pencoed†
Was a student who was studying Freud
The psychoanalysis
I can't say I miss
But the anal stage I quite enjoyed

Pontypridd

At a rainbow's end in Pontypridd‡
I searched for the gold underneath
But after hours of looking
All I found was some fucking
Old beer cans and a used rubber sheath

---

† Which can be pronounced in various ways, but we're relying on the pronunciation 'Pen-coyd' here.
‡ Pronounced 'Ponty-preeth'

Porthcawl

There was a young man from Porthcawl
Who had one extremely large ball
As if in compensation
For its close relation
His other was really quite small

Rhondda

Two young ladies I met in Rhondda
Gave me an awkward choice to ponder
They both stripped quite bare
Showed me their pubic hair
And asked me to judge which one was blonder

Swansea

There was a student from Swansea
Who went on an oral sex spree
By the end of term
She'd consumed so much sperm
She'd put on eleven stone three

Talbot Green*

A young man from Talbot Green
Once invented a fucking machine
Concave or convex
It would suit either sex
And jerked itself off in between

Powys

Brecon

There once was a young man from Brecon
Who said to me, 'Have you got a second?'
Then got out his chopper
Said, 'I think it's a whopper
But tell me frankly what do you reckon?'

Builth Wells

At a car boot sale they held in Builth[†]
On sale was some amazing filth
I parted with my cash
For a fantastic porn stash
Which I bought from the most charming milf

Crickhowell

In Crickhowell in the valley of Usk
All day long for loose change I did busk
I sang 'The Good Ship Venus'
Then got out my penis
But the responses to both were quite brusque

---

† Pronounced 'Bilth'

Hay-on-Wye

There once was a young man from Hay
Whose pubes overnight had turned grey
Then they all fell out
Which left him without
Till he invented the pubic toupee

Llandrindod Wells

One spring day in Llandrindod Wells
I did a painting in pastels
It depicted my manhood
And some flowers from the wood
I called it 'Penis with Bluebells'

Newtown

There was a couple from Newton in Powys
Who were quite into their golden showers
Their neighbours at night
Would face the common sight
Of them out pissing onto their flowers

Welshpool

A mystic from the town of Welshpool
Made a potion from out of toadstool
Which he said would grow his winky
Which was rather dinky
Until he was hung like a mule

South Glamorgan

Barry

I failed with my sex shop in Barry
That was the size of a cash and carry
All the shelves on the walls
I filled with Ben Wa balls
But supply and demand didn't marry

Cardiff

There was a young man from Cardiff
Who was such a big fan of Sir Cliff
If he heard just one play
Of 'Summer Holiday'
His dick would be rapidly stiff

Cowbridge

In Cowbridge in the Vale of Glamorgan
I went around driving a Morgan
A car of such class
Impressed this fair lass
Who was quickly impaled on my organ

Llantwit Major

In the Welsh town of Llantwit Major
I met this cantankerous old stager
Who said, 'I bet my dick's bigger
Than your little jigger'
But he ended up losing that wager

Penarth

A magician from the town of Penarth
Would try anything for a laugh
Till he failed with this trick
That he performed on his dick
Which just left his cock sawn right in half

West Glamorgan

Briton Ferry

With this young lady from Briton Ferry
My suggestion did not please her very
That she and her chums
Might fondle my plums
If I bought them all a round of sherry

Gorseinon

There was a chap from Gorseinon
Who was troubled by a terrible pong
His wife to him stated
The smell emanated
From the cheese that grew under his dong

Loughor

This chap said to me, once in Loughor[†]
'It's true that my wife is no looker
But I'm not gonna leave her
'Cause she's got a nice beaver
And twice a year she let's me fuck her'

[†] Pronounced approximately 'Lucker'

Neath[*]

There once was a mouse from Neath
That circumcised boys with its teeth
This wasn't for leisure
Or for sexual pleasure
But to get to the cheese underneath

Pontardawe

A young man from Pontardawe[‡]
Who bathed his dick in delay spray
Started wanking his member
On the fourth of December
And came on the fifteenth of May

Port Talbot

One night in Port Talbot, Glamorgan
They told me I exposed my organ
I can't really recall
Getting it out at all
But I'd drunk a lot of Captain Morgan

---

‡ Pronounced 'Pon-tar-dah-weh'

Northern Ireland

Antrim

Antrim

There was a young lady from Antrim
Who it's said had a rather large quim
She could use it to store
Ten dildoes or more
If she filled it right up to the brim

Ballyclare[*]

There was a chap from Ballyclare
Who was fucking his wife on the stair
As he quickened his stroke
The banister broke
So he finished her off in mid-air

Ballymena

A young man from Ballymena
Found a misuse for his vacuum cleaner
Of course it hadn't been made
As a masturbation aid
And caused lacerations to his wiener

Ballymoney

Whilst I was in Ballymoney
I ate only milk and honey
With no ill effects
Except going off sex
And finding my poo slightly runny

Belfast

At a urinal once in Belfast
I saw a sight that had me aghast
This chap had a dong
So handsomely long
I said, 'Sir, you have got mine out-classed'

Carrickfergus

This lass from Carrickfergus Marina
Seemed to be of such a nice demeanour
But her grip was so strong
As she played with my dong
She damn nearly tore off my wiener

Larne

A flatulent young man from Larne
Said, 'My farts are of so little charm
They're on Richter scale seven
Honk to high heaven
And they set off the flat's smoke alarm'

Lisburn

There once was a couple from Lisburn
Who fucked anywhere without concern
They would even have sex
In the middle of Next
And were quite often asked to return

Newtownabbey

A young lady I met from Newtownabbey
Said, 'I'm afraid that my pussy's quite scabby'
She had meant her feline pet
Which we took to the vet
Her snatch I found wasn't too shabby

Portrush

A young lady I met from Portrush
Said, 'OK I'll screw you at a push
But the state you must pardon
Of my lady garden
It's been months since I last trimmed my bush'

Armagh

Armagh

On a night out in the town of Armagh
I drank far too much Stella Artois
I can't really recall
What I did that night at all
But I awoke wearing panties and bra

Craigavon

A shop near the Craigavon lakes
Sells prophylactics of all makes
With a range that comprises
Fourteen shapes and sizes
To fit almost all trouser snakes

Lurgan

In Lurgan by the shore of Lough Neigh[†]
I was having a reasonable day
Till I read this book
That was as useless as fuck
It was titled 'Fifty Shades of Grey'

[†] The largest lake in Northern Ireland, pronounced 'Loch Nay'

Portadown

There was a young man from Portadown
With ejaculations that would astound
His come shot so high
It went up in the sky
And three miles away would touch down

Down

Banbridge

In Banbridge in County Down
Lived a young man of quite some renown
All the other lads
Were surprised at his 'nads
Which were oddly square and not round

Bangor

With my hosts when I stayed once in Bangor
I fear I dropped a slight social clanger
When they were looking for Dick
They had meant their son Rick
Misunderstanding, I got out my wanger

Carryduff

A young lady from Carryduff
Had a most versatile muff
She'd fill her furry taco
With chewing tobacco
Which it could grind into powdered snuff

Comber

There was a young man from Comber
Whose knob had the strangest aroma
It was said that even if
You took just one sniff
It could put you for weeks in a coma

Donaghadee*

A young lady from Donaghadee
Found herself with lots of time free
So she sat on the stairs
Counting her pubic hairs
And got to a thousand and three

Downpatrick

There was a young man from Downpatrick
With an unusual use for his dick
He put marks up one side
At gaps an inch wide
And used it as a measuring stick

Dundonald

For this town I struggled with the lines
To describe any sexual pastimes
For in truth with 'Dundonald'
Apart from the name 'Ronald'
There's not a word that fucking rhymes

Holywood

An injured pirate from Holywood
Said, 'This ship's surgeon's work is no good
His repair on my tackle
Is rather ramshackle
What use is this penis of wood?'

Kilkeel

A dominatrix from Kilkeel
Found a way to make me tunefully squeal
By whacking my cock
On various spots
With the hammers from her glockenspiel

Newcastle

In Newcastle in County Down
I went for a potter around
With my dick hanging out
And an occasional shout
Of, 'Who wants a suck for a pound?'

Newry

There was a young fellow from Newry
Who fancied some genital jewellery
And thought it mightn't much hurt
To do his own Prince Al-bert
In a moment of most utter foolery

Newtownards

A young man from Newtownards
Sent his lover a note with regards
Saying, 'Don't you be fearful
I'll keep myself cheerful
By the playing of pocket billi-ards'

Warrenpoint

A young man from Warrenpoint
Went every night to a strip joint
Then home he would race
At a fantastic pace
To give exercise to his wrist joint

Fermanagh

Enniskillen

One night a young man from Enniskillen
Thought that sex with goats would be thrilling
But he was all out of luck
Couldn't find a doe or buck
Let alone one that was willing

Lisnaskea

In Lisnaskea in County Fermanagh
At the offices of the town planner
Passing time whilst I waited
I gladly demonstrated
Photocopying my arse on his scanner

Londonderry

Coleraine

I had internet problems in Coleraine
With at last my connection regained
I caught up with my banking
And then with my wanking
Till all about me was quite semen stained

Derry

A sex worker I met in Derry
Said for the right price she might please me very
I said, 'That's a stickler[†]
All I've got's a French tickler
Three pounds and a bottle of sherry'

Limavady

The night I spent in Limavady
My behaviour was somewhat foolhardy
I remember being sick
After getting out my dick
But I had drunk a lot of Bacardi

[†] I was using the word 'stickler' in the sense of a noun meaning any
puzzling or difficult problem.

Magherafelt

A young lady from Magherafelt
Liked to whip me hard with a belt
But I soon felt the strain
Of quite so much pain
And my buttocks have still got a welt

Portstewart

There was a chap from Portstew-art
Who let rip the most enormous fart
With a velocity
Of approaching Mach three
Which gave him a bit of a start

Tyrone

Coalisland

In Coalisland near to Lough Neagh[†]
I upset the hosts for my stay
Their fancy bathroom suite
Had confused me a treat
And I'd took a dump in their bidet

Cookstown

There was a young man from Cookstown
Got erections while watching Countdown
He fancied Rachel Riley
So fucking highly
He just couldn't keep his dick down

Dungannon

When I was in the town of Dungannon
I was feeling quite lost and abandoned
Till this lass said to me
'If you like it with three
You could fuck me and my companion'

[†] As noted above, the largest lake in Northern Ireland, pronounced
'Loch Nay'

Omagh

A magician from the town of Omagh
Had an act that was strange and bizarre
He first produced a plectrum
From out of his rectum
Then pulled out from the same his guitar

Strabane

A chap to his wife from Strabane
Said, 'You know I'm not one to complain
But that's rather a meanness
To chop off my penis
'Cause I smiled at your sister Lorraine'

Index of Towns

A

ACKNOWLEDGEMENTS

Although none of them can or should be blamed for any of the limericks that appear here, a huge debt of thanks is owed to Jennifer Manson, Sarah Loving and Kevin Cross for all their help in various aspects of bringing this book to print.

Printed in Great Britain
by Amazon